Other published writings by Dr. David Schroeder

Follow Me: Discipleship by the Book (also in Spanish)
The Follow Me Group Guide (also in Spanish)
Matthew: The King and His Kingdom
The Broken God: Power Under Control
Ephesians: God's Grace and Guidance in the Church
Dadship and Discipleship: Character
Where It Counts Most
Pursuing the Glory of God: A Biography of Paul Bubna
Upfront Musings: Christ and Culture on the Campus
Walking in Your Anointing (also in Spanish)

Dr. Schroeder's monthly commentary, *Upfront,* has been circulated for over twenty years to an avid audience of readers from his various ministries.

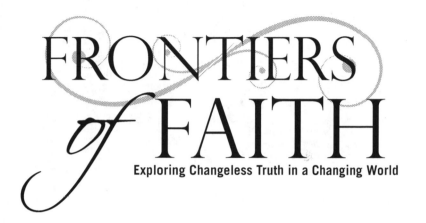

FRONTIERS of FAITH

Exploring Changeless Truth in a Changing World

DAVID E. SCHROEDER

authorHOUSE®

AuthorHouse™
1663 Liberty Drive
Bloomington, IN 47403
www.authorhouse.com
Phone: 1 (800) 839-8640

Published by AuthorHouse   04/25/2017

ISBN: 978-1-5246-7167-9 (sc)
ISBN: 978-1-5246-7166-2 (e)

Library of Congress Control Number: 2017902258

Print information available on the last page.

>New International Version (NIV)
Holy Bible, New International Version®, NIV® Copyright ©1973, 1978, 1984, 2011 by Biblica, Inc.® Used by permission. All rights reserved worldwide.

>New American Standard Bible (NASB)
Copyright © 1960, 1962, 1963, 1968, 1971, 1972, 1973, 1975, 1977, 1995 by The Lockman Foundation

>King James Version (KJV)
Public Domain

>English Standard Version (ESV)
The Holy Bible, English Standard Version. ESV® Permanent Text Edition® (2016). Copyright © 2001 by Crossway Bibles, a publishing ministry of Good News Publishers.

Contents

Section Three: The Spirit and the Church

Biographical Sketch of Dr. David E. Schroeder

Dr. David E. Schroeder is president of Pillar College, New Jersey's only accredited evangelical college, which he relocated to Newark to serve the inner-city, underserved populous. From 1993 to 2005 Dr. Schroeder was president of Nyack College (NY). During his leadership, the student population of the college and seminary more than tripled to over 3000. The Manhattan campus, a product of Dr. Schroeder's vision, began offering full degree programs in 1997, and by 2005 served over 1000 students.

A 1968 graduate of Nyack College, Dr. Schroeder was ordained in 1974 at the church he pastored in Armonk, NY. Dr. Schroeder has also pastored other churches in the United States and England. In addition to his B.A. in philosophy, Dr. Schroeder earned the M.A. in humanities from Manhattanville College, the S.T.M. from New York Theological Seminary and the Ed. D. from New York University.

His experience includes serving as VP for US Ministries for Trans World Radio from 1982-87, Executive Vice President and then President of Philadelphia

Theological (Reformed Episcopal) Seminary from 1988-91 and Director of Higher Education for The Christian and Missionary Alliance from 1991 until 1993 when he assumed the presidency of Nyack College. He was elected to serve as president of Alliance Theological Seminary beginning in September 2000.

He served on the C&MA board of directors for 8 years, and also on the boards of Atlantic Bridge, Overseas Ministry Study Center, Christian Herald, International Teams, Willow Valley Retirement Communities, The C&MA Fund, Arise and Walk Ministries Foundation, The Malachi Fund, Leadership for Development, Christ Church, the Fellowship Deaconry, and Pillar of Fire.

A frequent speaker at men's retreats, mission conferences, and seminars, David Schroeder's mission travel in recent years included Nigeria, the Philippine Islands, China, Lebanon, Holland, Belgium, Ukraine, Russia, Thailand, Cambodia, South Korea, Peru, Argentina, Zimbabwe, South Africa, Haiti, and the Dominican Republic.

In 1987 Dr. Schroeder began MasterWorks, Inc., a ministry that produces, distributes and teaches discipleship materials. His book *Follow Me: The Disciple-making Strategy of Jesus* and the companion *Follow Me Group Guide* have been used by scores of churches to foster strong discipleship ministries, and are now available in Spanish under the title *Sígueme.*

Dr. Schroeder and his wife Betzi have enjoyed ministering together for over forty years. They have three children and eight grandchildren, and reside in Middlesex, New Jersey.

Foreword for Frontiers of Faith

This is a book filled with good news—the good news that there is more than just information -- there is truth; Truth that we can hold on to, Truth that brings hope and change and offers a solid foundation to build our lives upon. Information can be helpful, but truth can actually bring freedom and life. Truth matters!

Belief shapes us; so in this book, David Schroeder helps our belief land solidly on truth—a truth that has been revealed through the Old and New Testament Scriptures and also revealed clearly in the person of Jesus Christ. This is a truth that ultimately can be written on our hearts, where it shapes and affects all that we are— mind, body and spirit.

David has written many helpful books, but this book is born out of his growing burden to help believers know that true faith is never blind, shallow, irrational or passionless. *Frontiers of Faith* introduces many important theological concepts, while also making these concepts accessible and understandable. The Christian faith is an evidence-based faith with strong historical and archeological support, but it is also a faith that should lead believers into reverence and awe, where both mind and heart are bowed together. The greatest commandment of God according to Jesus is that we **love the Lord with all of our heart, soul and mind (Matthew 22).** Emotion and passion can go beyond reason and intellect, but are never to be separated from them.

David Schroeder is many things. He is a loving husband, father and grandfather who cares deeply for his family. He is an effective leader who has been used to grow and transform many organizations. David is also a gifted teacher who energetically pours into learners and is strongly motivated to pass on life-changing truth not just information. But David is first and foremost a follower of Jesus who seeks to be authentic in his words and actions. David is also a good friend, and I have had the privilege of being his friend and serving alongside him in recent years.

Frontiers of Faith gives a solid introduction both of **what** to believe as revealed by scripture and the **reasons** to believe. It is a book of good news that will grow your understanding and your heart as a disciple of Jesus.

Rev. Rob Cruver
Founder of Urban Impact
Author of *The Blue Jeans Gospel*

Preface

During the past decade, a growing burden for me has been the erosion of biblical literacy and reverence. God has given me a great love for the younger generations, so my burden is not borne out of a need for them to adopt my generation's culture, but out of two concerns: the glory of God in the next generation of Christ-followers (reverence) and their well-being as people who are always most blessed as we conform to God's will and ways revealed in the Christian scriptures.

As a young boy growing up in Minnesota, I loved the wildness of the woods. I spent thousands of hours exploring the woods in the northern counties. This fixation was fueled by my love for reading about the American pioneers. Daniel Boone, Davy Crockett, Jim Bowie, Kit Carson, Wild Bill Hickok, Lewis and Clark, Buffalo Bill, Wyatt Earp, and a dozen others were my heroes. I longed to be part of that era when the western frontiers were being blazed. Exploring in other arenas besides the wild-west has continued as a lifelong pursuit. American cities, cultures of the world, the philosophies of the ages, and biblical truth continue to pump my adrenaline, so exploring my faith has become a passion.

My mission in writing *Frontiers of Faith* is to arouse and inform the faith of young believers and to deepen the faith of veteran Christians. Throughout the ages, Christians have taught the basics of Christian truth and faith in catechism or confirmation classes in church. Evangelicals moved away from these disciplines which in many churches had supplanted the emphasis on a personal salvation experience. Instead, in the past few centuries, young people (and sometimes adults) went to Sunday school, which often just repeated the same old Bible stories with advancing vocabulary and concepts. Taught mostly by wonderful but theologically uneducated lay men and women, Sunday school classes rarely delved deeply into theology. So, for many Christians, theology is an unexplored frontier. My hope is that this book will be a trustworthy guide for many into the primary paths of truth that are foundational for a Christian's faith.

Even though this volume lays out the basic beliefs of the Christian faith in twenty-first century language, this is not a comprehensive theology textbook. It is not meant primarily for the academic classroom, although it might serve as a useful supplementary text. I would be delighted if this book serves as a theology "primer," and many readers would move on to more substantial works such as Millard J. Erickson's *Introducing Christian Doctrine*[1] or Wayne Grudem's *Systematic Theology*.[2] My desire is to provide a resource that will help followers of Jesus Christ mature in core convictions, character, and competency as communicators of the Christian message. I'd like to hear of individuals who come to know what they believe about God and why faith in Jesus Christ is central to their lives.

Section One:
The Father and His Word

Chapter 1

Solid Rock Faith

Closing the greatest sermon ever delivered, Jesus said, ...*everyone who hears these words of Mine and acts on them, may be compared to a wise man who built his house on the rock. And the rain fell, and the floods came, and the winds blew and slammed against that house; and yet it did not fall, for it had been founded on the rock* (Matthew 7:24, 25). Unfortunately, the erosion of faith so evident today suggests that many people are building their lives on soft sand. Looking back over years of ministry, many faces come to my mind—people who seemed to have well-built houses of faith, but whose lives crumbled and faith faltered when the storms came. Others seemed always to be looking for an adequate foundation and never seemed to get around to building a life of faith.

In this "post-modern" age a new openness to the legitimacy of a life of faith is taking us out of the spiritual dark ages brought on by the so-called Enlightenment. Science, technology and progress have been shown to be a false trinity, and there is an increasing interest in an old science, once called "the queen of the sciences," theology.

Yes, theology. Once reserved for Bible colleges and seminaries, the study of theology is now going public, but with a different agenda than in previous days. In times past, theologians were absorbed with such ideas like how many angels can dance on the head of a pin. Today's emerging theologians are prophets and heralds who are challenging us to grapple not just with the doctrine of God but, more importantly, the person of God. They invite us to know intimately the God that others have been content only to know about, because more than an understanding is needed; a relationship is paramount. And as we understand experientially, we find ourselves building a rock-solid theology.

Reasonable Faith

Christian believers have a very strong foundation for building their faith and for promoting it with the greatest confidence. However, most Christians do not know how strong their position is. For generations, our society has forced an artificial divorce between faith and reason. Because many believers buy into that mentality, their faith is tentative and they are reluctant to be very public about it. By acknowledging that reason does not necessarily lead to faith, we have allowed the world to conclude incorrectly that faith is irrational. And a number of Christian thinkers from Tertullian ("I believe because it is absurd") to Kierkegaard ("Reason is the enemy of faith") have not helped us make the subtle, but important, distinction between *irrational* and *non-rational*. While faith is not based on reason alone, it is not irrational. In fact, faith is eminently reasonable. The truth is, as we will show later, every worldview is a faith worldview, even (especially) atheism.

Another false dichotomy we have accepted is the incompatibility between science and religion. We have allowed the secular world to demand that we play their game by their rules. Their rules are very narrow, requiring us to ignore the tentativeness of certain scientific theories and allowing for only a rigid interpretation of scriptural texts. So, when that rigid interpretation and an unproven theory conflict, the secular public gladly writes off religion as not being scientific, and, therefore, outdated.

But the twenty-first century offers a new approach to religion and faith – one that re-introduces the importance of theology. Post-modernism is rightly suspicious of the rigidity and narrowness of science. The progress we had expected from the enlightened application of science and technology has not materialized; indeed, the fruit of our enlightenment now threatens to turn the lights out permanently on planet Earth. The cold war has thawed, but the tools of destruction have been scattered and are now in the hands of people whom we fear to be irresponsible and mercenary. Many people think the issue is not *whether* a massive nuclear war will occur, but *when*. Sophisticated skeptics of religion are now turning toward some belief system that will help them feel safer and more significant. Thus, a whole new catalog of religious options is being formed, much of it under the umbrella term

New Age. Others, in their nervousness about adopting any particular religion, embrace them all. This is called pluralism. It is the ultimate tolerance – all roads lead to God, or the gods, or to a blissful life after death, if there is such a thing.

Perhaps it is good that people are becoming more sensitive to spiritual issues, but the seduction toward false belief is a strong siren. People who are new to Christian faith will not need to starve on an impoverished spiritual menu. On the contrary, they will need to learn to be selective in choosing what is healthy and what is harmful. Or to change the metaphor, they will need to learn the difference between solid rock theology and sinking sand religion. With that in mind, *Frontiers of Faith* is presented to help establish new believers and encourage veteran believers in the strength of the Christian faith.

Examining Faith

Nearly twenty-five hundred years ago, Socrates said, "An unexamined life is not worth living." A Christian paraphrase expresses a little different thought: "An unexamined faith is not worth having." Perhaps this is overstated, but in a very real sense, one who has faith in God is responsible to pursue an understanding of it. Or, more properly, of Him. God is not merely a subject to be understood, but a Person to be known. Theology is unlike all other areas of knowledge in that the author of the primary text invites learners not just to read his work, but to enter a personal relationship with Him.

One of the basic teachings of Christianity is that God Himself is the Source and Author of all truth. Christians never need to fear that any discovery will ever conflict with Christian truth. Being grounded in the Christian faith will give the believer full confidence that everything learned that is really true will add to his or her understanding of God and His ways. One of the presuppositions of Christian liberal arts colleges is that all truth is God's truth. So, we can boldly explore Christian theology, and even build our lives upon it.

One might wonder, "How important, really, is it for a lay person to know theology? Isn't theology just for the clergy?" In days past, we had that same attitude toward our health. People seemed content to leave everything in the hands of the doctor. Wise people today, however, know that no one is as motivated to care for their body as they are themselves. So, in my case, the more I know about blood pressure and cholesterol, the better quality of life I will lead (provided I act on that knowledge). Similarly, knowledge of basic theology is important for every person.

We all know that words can be rubbery, difficult-to-handle things. Just when you think you know the meaning of a word, it pops up in a new way so that you are not sure what it really does mean. Learning the meaning of words is like trying to hold a volleyball under water. It just wants to pop right back up to the top. That has always been the problem with meanings in language. Just when we think we have a definition "down," the word pops up meaning something else. For example, a generation ago the term *spirituality* was used exclusively to describe a Christian pursuit. Today the term is respectfully used in third force psychology, New Age religion, and eastern mysticism. Words can truly be slippery.

The early church fathers found that they had to state very carefully what the church actually believed about God the Father, Jesus Christ, and the Holy Spirit. In fact, not long after Jesus died, rose from death and ascended, false teachers travelled throughout Palestine and the Roman Empire teaching erroneous views about Jesus. Wherever the Apostle Paul went to minister and to establish Christian churches, groups of troublesome men would soon show up, working their way into the congregations to sow the seeds of wrong and harmful theology. Paul had to revisit these churches several times to make sure that they were on solid ground in their Christian faith.

The word for wrong teaching and belief is *heresy.* More than just false teaching, heresy actually means *truth that is out of balance.* Scripture teaches clearly, for example, that Jesus was fully God and fully man. But because that concept is difficult for our minds to understand, many began to teach that he only appeared to be man while really being only a spirit. Others took the opposite approach, saying that he only appeared to be God but he really was just a man. While both of these positions are partly true, neither is totally true. So, they are called heresies--truth out of balance.

Dr. A. W. Tozer wrote in *The Knowledge of the Holy,*[3] "What comes into our minds when we think about God is the most important thing about us." In other words, our understanding of who God is -- not our theoretical viewpoint but our working or living viewpoint -- reveals much about us. We tend to move in our lives toward our mental image of God. It is very important, therefore, that our idea of God corresponds as nearly as possible to the true being of God.

In ancient Canaan, the land which the Israelites were promised and commanded to posses, the worship of Baal and other gods and goddesses was prevalent, and involved immoral activities. The reason for that is easily understood. Those gods were the gods of fertility, so the worshippers became involved in all kinds of sexual immorality to celebrate fertility. Their view of their gods determined their behavior.

The Jews, on the other hand, having a better understanding of who the true God is and what he is like, lived by a very high ethical standard--higher than any other the world ever knew prior to the coming of Jesus Christ.

I remember meeting a friend whom I had not seen for years. We had attended the same church and summer camp. As boys, we both professed faith in Jesus Christ. Unfortunately, in his college years my friend chose to live contrary to Christian standards. As years passed and he continued to drift morally, his beliefs also changed. Decades later when we met again and talked about church, he said he might attend a Unitarian church "because they don't tell you how to live." The Unitarian view of God is vastly different from the God who presents Himself in the Bible.

One of the chapters of this book considers the reliability of the Bible, since so much of what we will say about reasonable faith is based on teachings in the Bible. But be assured, while the historical trustworthiness of the Bible can be substantiated, our faith is not in the Bible, but the God of the Bible, and that is a solid-rock place, a reasonable foundation for your faith.

Chapter 2

The God Question

Mrs. Johnson asked her Sunday school class, "What is faith?" A boy's hand shot up. "OK, Ben, tell the class what you think faith is." Without hesitation Ben replied, "Faith is believing what you know isn't true." Mrs. Johnson had her work cut out for her.

Ben was reflecting the fairly widespread view that what people believe can be sorted into two categories: there are those facts that can be proven and that we work with in our real, everyday life, and, then, there are those religious ideas that we just sort of accept, or at least allow, even though we don't really believe them. These ideas are like believing in UFO's. We know there are some folks who ardently believe in UFO's, but the mainstream of society ignores them, even though the movie industry is fueled by our fascination with the extra-terrestrial.

Our world is quite skeptical today about the prospect of knowing absolute truth, especially about spiritual matters, and rightly so. There is a slim line between knowledge and faith. It is not a bold, solid line, but a line nonetheless. This is a line that must be crossed if anyone wants to make sense out of life. The material world does not offer explanations about why humans exist, or why our existence matters so much. But almost everyone believes that life is significant. If life really is important, the reason lies beyond the mere provable facts that the world can accept. Science views life simply as brute fact. But the human mind wants to know more—more than science can answer.

While faith is not believing what you know isn't true; faith is believing what you cannot prove scientifically to be true. But faith does not require us to be unreasonable. We believe in a lot of things we cannot prove to be true, but they are reasonable. For example, do you believe in love? Prove that love exists.

You might tell about a father who risked his life by jumping into a raging river to save his drowning son, and say that's love. But you have merely pointed to the effects of love; you have not proven that such a thing as love actually exists. A cynical person may look upon that very loving act and believe the father had self-centered motivations.

So, we choose to believe many things we cannot prove because these ideas are reasonable explanations.

Unfortunately, because many people see science and religion as being incompatible, some Christians are skeptical of science. However, science and religion can work well together. Archaeological exploration is a science, and thousands of archaeological findings have supported the claims of religion and the validity of the Bible. Science is not an enemy of faith.

Before The Beginning

One day a boy was stretching his mind and his dad's by asking questions about the world: How big is it? How old is it? How did it get here? The father answered the last question by saying God created the world. The young philosopher came back with the most logical question: "But, dad, who created God?"

The father answered in frustration, not because it was a stupid question but because the conversation was getting beyond him: "No one created God; he has always existed."

Christians would rightly expect this answer, but it does not totally satisfy the curious mind. Indeed, who or what created God? Our scientifically oriented world requires a cause for every effect. But cause and effect can exist only within the dimension of time because the cause must always come *before* the effect. If time is part of the creation, presumably, whatever or whoever is responsible for the creation exists outside the boundaries of time. And that is exactly what theists believe about God. To paraphrase Anselm, an early theologian, God is "that Being than which an earlier cannot be conceived." Unless God is believed to be the uncaused Being or uncreated Creator, our thoughts go into an infinite regress, which leads nowhere.

Part of the definition of God is that he is the eternal, uncreated being. To ask who made him is to ask an absurd question. Asking who or what came before God is like asking, "What was the name of the horse that finished ahead of the winner in the Kentucky Derby?" The term "winner" rules out a predecessor at the finish line. The term *God* rules out a predecessor. If it is argued that this is begging the question, a counter question is in order: What is your more reasonable alternative for explaining creation? If an answer is given, then we are on the way to the infinite regress: Then what created that? And that? And so on.

The earliest citizens of planet Earth did not seem to doubt the idea of Supreme Being. Different civilizations had different images and names for that being,[4] but it was generally assumed that Someone was out there, Someone who was responsible for what is here. Only since the Enlightenment and the scientific revolution has the question of God's existence come to center stage. Earlier thinkers pondered the reality of God from the platform of faith; modern thinkers do so from the position of doubt.

Of course, this has generated numerous attempts to prove God's existence. None have absolutely succeeded in satisfying the general public, despite the good efforts of Anselm, Thomas Aquinas, and Immanuel Kant. The combined weight of their attempted proofs does not compel belief, but along with a few supporting planks they provide a platform that gives great credibility to the reasonableness of belief in the existence of God. These planks include evidences of life after death, including the resurrection of Jesus of Nazareth, universal cultural customs such as sacrifice and worship, the innate sense of right and wrong (conscience), and the earthly existence or visitation of spirit beings (angels and demons).

While their work may or may not reveal what they truly believe, scriptwriters of modern movies seem to be obsessed with the possibility of aliens and transcendent beings. Exploring human history: how did we get here? – human purpose: why am I here? – and human destiny: is there life after death? beg for a transcendent world view. No one escapes these questions.

Behold, The World!

Indeed, God is the supreme question. Although the majority of people believe in a supreme power or creator, those who doubt the existence of an eternal Being pose another question that we ought to consider: i*f there is such a Being, h*ow *do we know he is a **personal** God?*

To answer this question, we must begin with what is, or what we know exists. We are quite sure that we as people exist and that we live on a rather large piece of land called Earth. We observe trees, rocks, flowers, sheep, stars, clouds, and other people, and we do not doubt their existence. So, the young man's question leaps right out at us: How did all this stuff get here? In fact, how did I get here?

In pondering my own existence, I know my parents had something to do with my arrival, and that their parents gave them birth, and so on back to the first parents. In other words, we believe in cause-and-effect relationships. When we look at the world and all that is in it, we see an obvious effect that must have a sufficient cause.

As human beings, we know that man is the highest form of intelligence living on the earth, but we also know that no human being is genius enough to create mountains, trees, and sheep. Even if thousands of years ago there were more intelligent people, we know they were not smart enough to create themselves. We must therefore look for a cause that is greater than all of its effects. No object or being in the world is great enough to create the world, so we must look outside the world.

In previous generations, we could not look very far beyond our earth. Now, however, we send people into space for firsthand observation of our solar system and space beyond. The Soviet cosmonaut was truthful; he did not see God out of there. In fact, no life has yet been discovered in outer space. Of course, by *life* scientists mean physical life. They are not looking for God.

What kind of cause, then, could have created our world?

Ancient people never expected that the Creator could be seen. They assumed the Creator to be a spiritual being, not a material being. This spiritual being was understood to be all-powerful and eternal--a sufficient cause for the effects called earth and life.

One of the ways we know that God exits is that a creation needs a creator! We cannot doubt the reality of the creation; therefore, we cannot doubt the reality of a creator. We call this creator, God.

In the beginning God created the heavens and the earth. God saw all that He had made, and behold, it was very good. And there was evening and there was morning, the sixth day. Thus the heavens and the earth were completed, and all their hosts (Genesis 1:1, 31; 2:1).

Besides looking at the creation outside ourselves, we may also look inside ourselves. We know ourselves to be personal beings with consciousness of ourselves. Again, if the cause must be greater than the effects, we may rightly assume that the creator of conscious life also has the attribute of personhood, of self-awareness. To speak about God as a person is not the same as to say he is human. God is a person in the sense that he is a self-aware, individual being. We use the masculine pronoun because in the Bible one of his primary identities is Father.

Good And Bad: Just A Fad?

Another way we know that there is a God is by our built-in sense of good and bad. Every person comes into the world with a sense of right and wrong. Every group of people throughout history has had rules of conduct. The rules may vary from one society to the next, but basically, they have the same foundation—to manage behavior for the common good. Some people say these are arbitrary rules. Others believe some of the rules are divinely given laws that pertain to all people. One thing is undeniable; we all have a sense of personal rights and justice. To convince a skeptic about the reality of morals who would have to deny that stealing is inherently wrong, one needs only to steal his car and see how he reacts!

Our sense of morality is reflected in our values. We place different values on different parts of creation. For example, we cut blades of grass every time we mow the lawn, and we do not feel guilty about it. We do not, however, cut the heads off other people if we feel they are getting too tall! We know that would be wrong. No one needs to tell us that. We do not even need to know the law to know it would be wrong. Human beings are not the same as grass; we value human beings much more than grass. It is right to cut tall grass, wrong to cut tall humans.

Why do we think humans have such high value? Who says people are worth more than plants? How did we get a sense of good and bad? Is not such thinking merely a social invention, as some people think, a mere fad that has existed for a few thousand years to help us get along better socially?

Part of our human equipment is the conscience, which gives us our instinctive morality. Consciences can be twisted, seared and perverted, but the reality of the conscience cannot be denied. There is something inside each human being that registers "good" or "bad", "right" or "wrong" when we are interacting with others. The human conscience is part of the image of God, built into every human being. And God has programmed that conscience with certain universal, absolute notions of morality, such as the value of human life.

Remember what the serpent said to Eve when tempting her to eat the forbidden fruit? *For God knows that in the day you eat from it your eyes will be opened, and you will be like God, knowing good and evil* (Genesis 3:5). The serpent was right about that.

We know good and evil because there is a morally focused God who has put this knowledge within us. Some of his attributes are moral attributes. For example, God is righteous and good. Our consciences are strong evidence for God's existence.

If there were no God, what difference would it make how I behaved? Oh, human authorities might punish me, but any clever person can find ways to break the law and get away with it. But only the most foolish think they are scot-free just because they have eluded human authority. Most thoughtful people realize the truth of Hebrews 9:27, ...*And inasmuch as it is appointed for men to die once and after this comes judgment.*... Our sense of having to give account of ourselves someday is also evidence of the existence of the judge of the universe whom we call God.

Every Head Bowed

Another clue of God's existence is the universal instinct to worship some form or idea of God or gods. Archaeologists and anthropologists have never discovered evidences of a society of people, ancient or modern, who were not worshipers. True, not all individuals have chosen to worship something outside of themselves. And some groups have worshiped the sun or a mountain or carved idols, but all cultures have been worshipping societies.

Rocks, plants, and animals do not worship, but God has created humans to be worshipers. Either we are wired wrongly or there is a God who is both the Source and Subject of our worship. People who say they do not worship have educated (or dis-educated) themselves into not worshipping, or, more likely, they really worship humanity. Nonetheless, they have a god, even if they refuse to call it that. Humans are instinctively and impulsively worshippers.

Eyes Of Faith

Another way of knowing about the reality of God is to heed the wise words of Hebrews 11:6, *And without faith it is impossible to please Him, for he who comes to God must believe that He is and that He is a rewarder of those who seek Him.* In other words, the person who does not want to believe in God is not a good candidate for receiving the knowledge of God's existence, but the person who wants the truth and who seeks God will be rewarded in his search if he starts in faith.

We cannot see germs without the help of a microscope. Suppose a child is told to wash her hands before eating, and she replies, "Why?" Her mom says, "To remove the germs." "I can't see any germs," she says, "so my hands are clean." The mother persists, "Well, even if you can't see them, they are there." If the girl continues not to believe in germs, an exceptionally patient parent might bring out a microscope, prepare a slide, and have her look through the lens. If the child really wants the truth, *by faith* she will look into the microscope. Faith is the microscope that "sees" God. If the child, however, enjoys her dirty hands too much to be bothered by truth, she will refuse to look into the microscope. So it is with people who do not want to believe in God.

God has given plenty of evidence of his existence. His "fingerprints" are all over His work. We see compelling evidence of God's reality through creation, our sense of morality, and the instinct to worship. And there is more – so much more – that we will see that it truly is difficult not to believe in God's reality because it is so reasonable.

Chapter 3

God the Communicator

Nearly every Jewish worship service begins with this call: *Hear, O Israel: The Lord our God, the Lord is one* (Deut. 6:4). From God's earliest communications we know that he is a unity. Nevertheless, in ancient times, and even today in some areas, people believed in many gods. The Greeks had their *pantheon*, a whole family of gods, each one specializing in something. There was a god of war, a goddess of love, a god of light, a god of wind, and many other gods in the pantheon. Hinduism believes in about three million gods. In fact, the idea of only one God was considered quite strange in ancient times. The Hebrews were considered to be strangely irreligious because of their monotheism – their belief in only one God.

The God of the Hebrews and the Christians differs from other so-called gods. The definition of the Judeo/ Christian God does not allow for other gods since he is unique as the Creator God. Even if there were other gods, they would have to have been created by the Creator God, so they would not have been anything like the true God. None of the gods ever conceived by the human mind possessed the attributes or abilities of the one God which Jews and Christians worship. These man-made gods have limited power and knowledge, but the one true God has unlimited power and knowledge. We know this, not because we imagined it, but because God has revealed his nature to us.

The true God also has revealed himself as a multi-dimensional Being. He is not just a force or a power; He is not the All, or even the Force. He has revealed himself as one God in three persons: Father, Son, and Holy Spirit. This is not to say that there are three gods, but rather that God reveals himself as one God, having one will, and having all abilities and attributes in his oneness. The fact that he is infinite suggests that all else is subordinate to him. When Satan, who was one of God's highest angels, tried to make himself equal with God, God cast him out of his presence. Nothing and no one can be God except God! And he has said,

> *You shall have no other gods before Me.*
> *You shall not make for yourself an idol, or*
> *any likeness of what is in heaven above or*
> *on the earth beneath or in the water under*
> *the earth. You shall not worship them*
> *or serve them; for I, the Lord your God,*
> *am a jealous God, visiting the iniquity of*
> *the fathers on the children, on the third*

> *and the fourth generations of those who hate Me, but showing lovingkindness to thousands, to those who love Me and keep My commandments* (Exodus 20:3-6).

God Has Spoken

Since God is personal, unique and immanent, it is reasonable that he would communicate with his creation and creatures. He communicates in a variety of ways. We are told that *the heavens are telling of the glory of God* (Psalm 19:1), a reference to Natural Revelation. A more Personal Revelation has come in the living Word, Jesus Christ (John 1:1). And God has also spoken in the written Word, the Bible, which because he is its primary source, we believe the Bible was inerrant in its original transmission. Often, the written Word is called Special Revelation. So, we have at least three kinds of communication from God: Natural Revelation (nature), Personal Revelation (Jesus Christ), and Written Revelation (the Bible). Other communications from God, such as dreams, prophecies, manifestations of the Spirit, guidance, and so on, are really not revelations in the same sense since they are not universal and timeless (for all people).

In the written Word, we are clearly taught that there is no other God: *To you it was shown that you might know that the Lord, He is God; there is no other besides Him* (Deut. 4:35). Israel was shown dramatically that there is only one God. Remember the contests between Moses and Pharaoh of Egypt? God showed clearly that whatever the Egyptians were worshipping as deity was not truly God. The miraculous way God delivered the Israelites and defeated the Egyptians left a deep impression on the Hebrews for centuries. Years later, when some of the Jews were worshipping the idols of Canaan, the Lord again showed that he is the only God. Elijah met 450 prophets of Baal on Mount Carmel to determine who was the true God. A contest was arranged so that the god who would drop fire from heaven would be proclaimed the true God. Elijah's God answered with fire (1 Kings 18:20-40). Baal did not.

God's Word reveals another conclusive proof that God is the only deity. That proof is Jesus Christ, God in the flesh. Now if a man came along making sensational claims, we would be free to believe him or not believe him if he were only a man. But, if he claimed to be from God, and in fact, to be the Son of God, and then he died and rose from the dead, we would be wise to believe he must know what he was talking about. Well, Jesus did just that. He told us about the one true God. To a woman he met at Jacob's well He said, *God is spirit, and those who worship Him must worship in spirit and truth* (John 4:24). Notice He did not say "their" worshipers. Either there is only one God, or else Jesus Christ, who was later raised from the dead, was a liar.

We Can Know God

How is God knowable? We have already established that there is a God, only one God, and that he is a personal being. From interacting with other human beings, we know that it is possible to know other beings. It must be possible, therefore, to know God. But, on the other hand, God is not just another being; He is infinite, eternal, mysterious, and totally spiritual. All the other beings we know do not have these attributes.

Usually when we speak about knowing someone, we mean that we have met face to face, and have spoken with one another. We cannot honestly talk about knowing God in that sense, for we have not seen him, nor have we had an audible discussion with him in which our ears have heard his voice.

We can still say, however, that we know God, for in fact, one of God's greatest criticisms of his backslidden people in Hosea's time was that they no longer knew him. Not only can we know God; he expects us to know him!

Have you ever met anyone who said he would believe if only he could see God? Such a statement totally misses one of the most basic truths about God – that he is a spirit. Our physical eyes do not have the capacity to see spirits. Since God is spirit, it is certain that if we are going to know him, it will have to be on his terms. Only as God reveals himself to us will we know him.

One of his terms is that only eyes of faith, not eyes of flesh, will see him. If we refuse to see God with eyes of faith, not eyes of flesh, we will not see him. The good news is that God has chosen to be known by those who will look for him with eyes of faith. God has left his "fingerprints" all over the universe. The apostle Paul wrote, *For since the creation of the world His invisible attributes, His eternal power and divine nature, have been clearly seen, being understood through what has been made, so that they are without excuse* (Romans 1:20). The word *men* in the last part of the verse refers to all mankind, even those who do not know God through the Bible. They are without excuse for not knowing God, for the evidence of his presence is all around us.

In my house, I have a beautiful set of books written by Charles Dickens. Over the years, I have read those books. If someone were to ask me if I knew Charles Dickens, I would answer with a qualified yes. Since he died in 1870, I obviously did not know him personally, but through his works I have grown to know much about him. Certainly, I could never doubt his existence. To do so, I would have to explain his excellent books in some other way.

Similarly, although I have never seen God in the flesh, I know much about him by his work. Certainly, I cannot doubt his existence because his work is so evident. When in the next life I see God in a more literal sense, he will not be a stranger to me; I have known him even though I have not yet seen him.

Through God's handiwork we can only know about him, but our greater need is to know God personally. That is possible *because that which is known about God is evident within them; for God made it evident to them* (Romans 1:19). The words *what may be known* come from one Greek word, pronounced *knowstone*. The *knowstone* is the knowable of God; it is almost like an organ in our body used specially to pick up and record deity-waves. Every person has the ability to know God. This knowledge is not just the *know-about* kind of knowledge, but the *know-personally-through-experience* kind of knowledge.

Some call this *knowstone* the conscience; others call it the soul or the spirit, but whatever it is called, God has given us all a built-in knowability of himself. Those who refuse to use their *knowstone* are as foolish as is a man who would not use electricity just because he cannot see it or understand it.

We all know that an important part of knowing someone is communicating with him. God, being a Person, has provided a way for us to communicate with him, and in that way we may know him also. Paul, the apostle, spoke about *but just as it is written, "Things which eye has not seen and ear has not heard, And which have not entered the heart of man* (1 Corinthians 2:9). Then he goes on to say, *God revealed them through the Spirit; for the Spirit searches all things, even the depths of God* (1 Corinthians 2:10). How is God knowable? By his Spirit communicating with our spirit. *We have received...the Spirit who is from God, so that we may know the things freely given to us by God (v. 12).* Our spiritual ears are able to pick up those divine sound waves that tell about God's reality. Romans 8:16 says it this way: *The Spirit Himself bears witness with our spirit that we are children of God.*

Only those with a spirit alive to God's Spirit will hear that message, but God is definitely knowable through this Spirit-to-spirit communication!

All these ideas about God's existence, cause and effect, worship instincts, God's personalness, and knowing God are important, but useless if we do not get to know God personally. Throughout this book, you will learn much about God, but that is not enough. We must come to know him personally, and just as meeting another person occurs at a specific time, so does meeting God.

We start a personal relationship with him when we are willing to meet him on his terms. We will be talking about those terms in coming chapters, but make sure the one thing you remember from this chapter is that God is knowable on a personal level; it is not good enough just to know about God!

Chapter 4

Being and Behavior Attributes

Looking at the various characteristics of God, we are at once aware of the impossibility of describing God adequately, even by using an infinite number of words. A hymn writer of the seventeenth century penned these words:

> *Oh God, Thou bottomless abyss!*
> *Thee to perfection who can know?*
> *O height immense! What words suffice*
> *Thy countless attributes to show?*[5]

The writer correctly understood that God's attributes themselves are countless, so our discussion of his attributes will be only representative. The attributes of God may be considered in two categories. First, we will look at what might be called *being* attributes and then at the *behavior* attributes. Theologians use more complex terms: *incommunicable* and *communicable* attributes, meaning those we cannot even imitate and those we can imitate on a finite level.

Being attributes are those qualities of God that have to do with who he is. We will look at four. The first is that God is **self-existent**. He is uncreated and independent of his creation. John 5:26 indicates this: *For just as the Father has life in Himself, even so he gave to the Son also to have life in Himself.*

Theologians use the word *aseity* to describe the fact that God is totally independent of all other beings. He has life in himself and can perfectly exist without any of his creation. When we speak of God being eternal, we are not saying that God has lived a very long time but are affirming that God lives outside the boundaries of time and, therefore, is not subject even to the dimensions of space and time. While this is very abstract thinking, it is nonetheless true that God is wholly independent of anyone or anything else. He is self-existent.

Second, God is **infinite**. The best way to understand this attribute is to refer to its opposite, a word that we can understand – *finite*. Since *finite* means "with limitation," *infinite* means not having any limitation.

There are many ways in which God is infinite. We think immediately of three "omni's." God is *omnipotent*, that is, all-powerful. *For nothing will be impossible with God* (Luke 1:37). There is no limitation to his power. He is *omniscient*, that is, all-knowing. There is no limitation to God's knowledge. Nothing in all creation is hidden from God's sight. *All things are open and laid bare to the eyes of Him with whom we have to do* (Hebrews 4:13).

He is *omnipresent*, that is, everywhere present at once. There is no limitation to his presence. *Where can I go from Thy Spirit? Or where can I flee from Thy presence?* (Psalm 139:7). That is what we mean when we say God is infinite, but God is infinite in many other ways as well.

A third being attribute is that God is **immutable**. He does not change. Any change would be a movement away from perfection. James 1:17 supports this idea: *Every good thing bestowed and every perfect gift is from above, coming down from the Father of lights, with whom there is no variation, or shifting shadow.* For him to change would be to become un-God. A. W. Tozer suggested that for a moral being to change, the change would be in one of three directions. He would have to go from better to worse, from worse to better, or if his moral quality would remain stable, he must change within himself as from immature to mature or from one order of being to another. Obviously, God's perfection would not allow any such possibility of change.

The fact that God is unchangeable ought to be very comforting to us. Imagine the fear we would experience if we were subject to a ruler who had violent mood swings. We would never know whether to expect his wrath or his love. But we know that God always loves his creatures and that his wrath is always against sin. Those things about God never change, nor does anything else about God ever change.

The last of the being attributes we are considering is that God is *personal*. It is conceivable to think of an impersonal god-like being – just a force to be reckoned with. People who are deists believe in a supreme Power, which was responsible for creation, but this Power is an impersonal energy rather than a being. God, however, has revealed himself as a personal being. In fact, we as persons are created in his image. *And God created man in His own image, in the image of God He created him: male and female He created them* (Gen. 1:27). This verse indicates that human beings are not the definition or prime example of personhood; God is. We are reflections of him.

Behavior Attributes

When we use the word *behavior* to describe attributes, we are not suggesting a moral quality as in a mother telling her little boy to behave himself. God's actions are always right and good. Behavior attributes speak of how God acts. Let us look at four of God's behavior attributes to help us understand how God acts.

God's **sovereignty** is that attribute by which he reigns supreme in total authority over all his creation. Whenever the Bible uses the name *Lord* in speaking about God, it is affirming the sovereignty of God; he has total freedom to make choices in the ruling of his universe. Another biblical title suggests God's sovereignty; he is *King of Kings.* Can you imagine a huge host of great kings who have ruled over large parts of the earth from the beginning of history, assembling together before one King who is over them all? That King could only be the God whom we have come to know and the God who has revealed himself through the Bible as sovereign.

Another of the behavior attributes is God's **holiness**. In fact, the holiness of God is one of the most basic qualities that separate God from his creation. *Holy* means absolutely without sin. It means *separate, distinct, unique.* While we creatures of God can strive for holiness, especially as we depend on Christ's holiness to make us righteous, no one other than God can be described as absolutely holy.

God expects his people to *be holy; for I am holy* (Leviticus 11:44). God did not say, "Be holy as I am holy," for that would be to demand absolute holiness. Both Isaiah in the Old Testament and Peter in the New Testament have given a glimpse of their understanding of holiness. In Isaiah chapter 5, the prophet proclaims woes on many people. Then in the sixth chapter he is in the temple and sees a vision of God. His response is a sudden awareness of his own unholiness, and he cries out, *Woe is me!...I am ruined! Because I am a man of unclean lips, and I live among a people of unclean lips; For my eyes have seen the King, the Lord of hosts* (Isaiah 6:5).

Peter saw his unholiness during one of his first meetings with Jesus, when the Lord had him go out deeper into the sea to catch many fish after a long night of unprofitable fishing. Peter's response was *Depart from me, for I am a sinful man, O Lord!* (Luke 5:8).

In other words, complete holiness is God's alone. In *The Knowledge of the Holy,* A. W. Tozer states, "Holy is the way God is. To be holy He does not conform to a standard. He is that standard."[6]

A third behavior attribute is God's **love**. Again, we should understand that love is not something that God has in some degree, but rather, that *God is love* (1 John 4:8). God's love is the attitude he has toward his creation. His primary attitude and actions are benevolent. After the sixth day of creation, God looked upon what he had made and he considered it to be very good, (Gen. 1:31). Despite the entrance of sin into the world through the disobedience of our first parents, we have no scriptural evidence that God reversed his opinion. The best-known verse in the Bible, John 3:16, says, *God so loved the world*, and he has continued to express that love as seen in the fact that *He gave His only begotten Son.*

The word used in the New Testament to describe God's love is *agape.* That Greek word refers not to a feeling, but to action. The acts that God undertakes in his created world are acts of love. This is not to say that he is not also a God of justice, an attribute that we will also consider. Rather, it is to say that whatever God does, comes from a motive of love. As we will see, even acts of justice which appear to have negative consequences stem from love.

C. S. Lewis has suggested that even sending unrepentant sinners to hell is a loving act, as explained this way. The highest dignity God can bestow upon a creature is individual will. Humans have not been created as automatons or robots. Apart from our sin, we are superior to the angels because God has given us the ability to make choices for him or against him. In a sense, we have a measure of sovereignty, which God will not violate. He loves humans so much that he will not force them to worship him or love him.

The unrepentant sinner who defies God, who refuses to submit to God, would be extremely uncomfortable in the immediate presence of God. In fact, the only thing more painful for the sinner than hell would be to be in heaven in an unrepentant state. Even though *God is now declaring to men that all everywhere should repent* (Acts

17: 30), he will allow people to disobey, but they will suffer the consequences of disobedience, namely, removal from the presence of God. We all know what it is like to have to face a person whom we have disobeyed. It is most uncomfortable to be in his or her presence until we have repented adequately. So, by this line of reasoning, God's casting the unrepentant sinner out of his presence is, in fact, acting in love rather than in vengeance. Hell is where God is not present, and that is the only place where an unrepentant, disobedient person can be without being in God's presence.

Of course, the unrepentant sinner might say if God truly loved him, God would not punish him for disobeying. Any parent would quickly see the absurdity of this idea. And in this case, it is even more absurd than in the family, because the only reason to disobey God is to try to be our own god, and God knows what lousy gods we make of ourselves.

You might think, well, why doesn't God just eliminate unrepentant sinners? Why subject them to eternal torment? Some people believe this idea called the doctrine of annihilation. It certainly is appealing because it makes God appear to be more civil, but it is false from two points of view: 1) Scripture indicates repeatedly that hell and its inhabitants are eternal, and 2) since we are created in the image of God, the human soul is eternal. If we were able to be annihilated, we would not be human.

The fourth behavior attribute, God's *justice*, refers to a moral standard of equity or fairness. In fact, the word *iniquity*, a synonym for sin, is actually the word *inequity*, the absence of equality in human thoughts and acts. When

God acts in justice, he is acting on the basis of a standard that he himself is and has set. Justice is not something outside of God, to which he must conform, but rather he himself is the standard of justice. Most simply, it means that God will always do the right thing, as shown in Psalm 33:4-5; *For the word of the Lord is upright; And all His work is done in faithfulness. He loves righteousness and justice; The earth is full of the lovingkindness of the Lord.*

The justice and love of God came together in the crucifixion of Jesus Christ. There we see God, who loves the world intensely and loves his only begotten Son, taking dramatic steps to bring people to himself without compromising what is right. He has not just winked at the sins or inequities of the world, but he has dealt thoroughly, yet lovingly, with them.

Other attributes of God are goodness, grace, mercy, faithfulness, wisdom, and majesty. We shall, however, move on to the next topic to allow you to find out for yourself what you can about those attributes of God. It is all part of coming to know what God is like – a lifelong and joyful task for the Christian!

Chapter 5

The Tri-Unity

God has revealed himself in three persons—Father, Son, and Holy Spirit. Throughout the centuries of church history various people and groups have challenged the fact that God is one God and yet three persons. The earliest Christians held this doctrine and were put in a most awkward position. The Gentiles, who believed in many gods, considered the Christians to be atheists because they did not believe in their gods. Jews, on the other hand, who were not persuaded that Jesus was the messiah, the Son of God, called the Christians pagans because they said the Christians believed in three gods. What both the Gentiles pagans and the non-Christian Jews found objectionable was the doctrine of the Trinity.

Modern people seem to have a great need to explain everything rationally. In our scientific era, we have learned to explain many here-to-fore perplexing mysteries. For example, we understand the rotation of the earth and the phenomenon of various seasons of weather. We also understand more about the human body than the ancients could possibly have known. We have unlocked many of the mysteries of nature.

The key to unlocking the mystery of the nature of God, however, has not been given to mankind. God is mysterious. He is incomprehensible. He is inscrutable. The full knowledge of what God is like is beyond the capacity of our minds. If we could fully understand God, we would be equal with him rather than be subject to him. From the very outset, let us fix it in our minds that the doctrine of the Trinity of God is not logically consistent with human thought patterns, and the exact nature of the triune God himself remains for us clouded in much mystery. But this inability is consistent with what we see in nature. Lower beings do not have the capacity to explore the depths of higher beings. Bears have offered nothing to our understanding of the human psyche, and we doubt that ants have much to contribute about bears.

After many struggles with heretical groups, Christians in the fourth century developed a creed that affirms the fact that God is *one substance* which can be known and identified in *three different persons*. This sounds quite abstract, so let us use an analogy. Though all analogies are inadequate, the best one to help explain the idea of the Trinity may be the chemical compound H20, known commonly as water. H_2O can be found in three distinctly different forms, all of which can be reduced again to H_2O.

We most commonly know H_2O in its liquid form, water. If water is heated to 100 degrees Centigrade or 212 degrees Fahrenheit, the H2O takes the form of a gas called steam. If water is cooled to 0 degrees Centigrade or 32 degrees Fahrenheit, the H2O takes the form of a solid called ice. Nonetheless, regardless of which of the three forms it is in –water, steam, or ice—it remains H2O.

So it is with the Trinity. Whether we are talking about Father, Son, or Holy Spirit, we are still talking about God.

Is It Bible-Based?

So far, what we have said about the Trinity is clearly theological. The pressing question is this: is it a biblical idea? Does the Bible support the fact that God is three persons with one nature?

There is no single passage in the Bible where the Trinity concept is developed fully or explicitly. There are, however, literally hundreds of references to the fact that God exists in the forms of the Father, Son, and Holy Spirit. When we study the Bible and explore doctrine, we must take all that the Bible says and not just focus on one small passage. So, it is actually more fortunate that we have many references to the Trinity rather than one extended teaching on it. The doctrine of the Trinity is strongly supported by looking at biblical references to the being of God and the works of God.

Earlier we discussed the attributes of God. If Father, Son, and Holy Spirit are all God, then all three persons share in the attributes of God. If any one of the persons of the Trinity does not have one of the attributes the others have, that part would not be God. Father, Son, and Holy Spirit, therefore, must all share in the attributes of God. At the end of this chapter you will find a helpful chart with

Scripture references that allude to attributes of God found in Father, Son, and Holy Spirit. The four being attributes and four behavior attributes that we have considered are used to show that the Trinity concept is, in fact, biblically based. As an illustration, let us focus on the infinity of God as found in all three persons of the Trinity.

All three persons of the Godhead are omnipresent. The omnipresence of God the Father is affirmed in Jeremiah 23:24 where God himself declares: *"Can a man hide himself in hiding places, So I do not see him?" declares the Lord. "Do not I fill the heavens and the earth?" declares the Lord.* The same truth about the omnipresence of God the Son is evident in Matthew 28:20. These are among the last words Jesus uttered while living on the earth: *and lo, I am with you always, even to the end of the age.* The omnipresence of God the Holy Spirit is evident in Psalm 139:7. David asked, *Where can I go from Thy Spirit?* As the psalmist continues, he mentions several rather remote places and in each case says, *You are there.* Omnipresence is an attribute shared by the Father, Son, and Holy Spirit. So it is with all of the attributes.

Saved By The Three

The attributes are one area where the Trinity is substantiated; the works of God are another area. One of the works of God in which Father, Son, and Holy Spirit all share is the salvation of believers. In this instance, we will look at three Scriptures, all written by one author. John 1:13 affirms that those who are saved are *born of God.* God the Father has an active role in the salvation of believers. John 1:12 refers to the role of God the Son in salvation by stating that, *but as many as received Him, to them He gave the right to become children of God.* In John 3, while discussing the means of salvation with a very important religious leader, Jesus emphasized the role of the Holy Spirit: *Truly, truly, I say to you, unless one is born of water and the Spirit, he cannot enter into the kingdom of God* (John 3:5). He went on to compare the work of the Holy Spirit with the wind that blows around us, which we hear but cannot see, and then he said, *so is everyone who is born of the Spirit* (John 3:8). The Father, Son, and Holy Spirit all participate in the work of salvation. The three are one not only in who they are but also in what they do, as seen below.

Works Of The Trinity

Works of God	Father	Son	Holy Spirit
Creation	Ps. 102:25	Col. 1:16	Gen. 1:2
Inspiration	2 Tim. 3:16	1 Pet. 1:10-11	2 Pet. 1:21
Birth of Christ	Gal. 4:4	Heb. 10:5	Luke 1:35
Salvation of Believers	John 1:13	John 1:12	John 3:5-8
Indwelling of Believers	Eph. 4:6	Col. 1:27	1 Cor. 6:19
Protection of Believers	John 10:29	John 10:28	Eph. 4:30
Presence for Witnessing	2 Cor. 3:5-6	1 Tim. 1:12	Acts 20:28

Man Is A Clue

One of the subtle ways the Trinity concept is supported in Scripture is the way God has made us in his own image. You may recall the Scripture where God, speaking within himself, said, *Let Us make man in Our image, according to Our likeness* (Gen. 1:26). Since God is a threefold being, we should not be surprised to find that we who are created in his image are also threefold beings. As human beings, we are composed of body, soul, and spirit. (See 1 Thessalonians 5:23.) We are unique in that regard in God's universe. Looking at other forms of life, we see that they are not created in God's image.

Plants, for example, have only body, and with it the plant relates to its immediate environment, the earth.

Animals have body and soul. Soul is the combination of intellect, will, and emotions. With body and soul, animals communicate only with the earth and their own peers. The higher forms of animal life seem to have more "soul."

Humans, however, have body, soul, and spirit, and thus communicate with our immediate environment (the earth) through our body, with peers (other people) through our soul; and with God through our spirit. Therefore, to come to the conviction that God is a threefold being, we may look within ourselves to see that we who are created in his image are also "little trinities."

Knowing Him

By examining the attributes of God and the Trinity of God, we learn much about God. We will continue to learn much more about him as we study his book, the Bible, directly. As important as it is to know about God, it is eternally more important to know God personally. Since one of his attributes is that all three persons of the Trinity are personal, it certainly would dishonor God to treat him only as a subject to be studied.

Theology is not like biology where you dissect an animal to examine all its parts to come to an intellectual knowledge of the subject. Rather, the only way to know

God is through having a personal relationship with him. Knowing about God is more harmful than helpful if you never get to know him personally, for we are accountable for that knowledge. It is far better to love God than just to learn about God. We will go on to explore how he has made it possible for us to know him and to love him.

Attributes Of The Trinity

Being Attributes	Father	Son	Holy Spirit
Self-existent	Ex. 3:14, 15	John 8:58	Gen. 1:2
Infinite	Jer. 23:24	Matt. 28:20	Ps. 139:7
Immutable	Mal. 3:6	Heb. 13:8	Heb. 9:14
Personal	Mal. 2:10	John 1:14	John 14:26

Behavior Attributes	Father	Son	Holy Spirit
Sovereign	Isa. 46: 10	1 Tim. 6:15	1 Cor. 12:11
Holy	Rev. 4:8	Luke 1:35	Ps. 51:11
Love	John 13:6	John 15:9	Gal. 5:22
Just	Ps. 89:14	Zech. 9:9	John 16:8

Chapter 6

The Father's Word

If God is a personal being, and if he cares about humans, and if he is able to communicate – three ideas we have already affirmed – then it makes sense that he will have found a way to express himself. In fact, he may have many ways to communicate with people. The word *revelation* refers to any process by which God makes something known to humans either about himself, his activity, or his will. God has revealed himself in several different ways, but especially in the three ways we discussed in chapter three.

We noted that everyone receives *Natural revelation* through which God makes himself known in nature or creation. The Psalmist says, *The heavens are telling of the glory of God; And their expanse is declaring the work of His hands* (Ps. 19:1). But we don't need the Psalmist to tell us that; all creation screams out that a powerful, intelligent Creator exists.

We also discussed *Personal revelation* in which God has spoken through a person, a specific person, his son Jesus Christ, who became a human person. In John 1 Jesus is introduced as the *Word*. He came as a full expression of God's message to humanity; he is the only personal revelation of God. Several chapters of this book are devoted to the personal revelation of God through Jesus Christ, but we would know nothing about that if God had not ensured that it was preserved for all time by providing a written revelation, the Bible, God's prepositional revelation, which is the main topic of this chapter.

Propositional revelation is God speaking through the words or writings of humans. *Proposition* merely means statement. The prophets and apostles were usually the agents of this kind of revelation. Ezekiel provides a good example: *The word of the Lord came to me* (Ezek. 7:1). In fact, the phrase *word of the Lord* (or combination of these words) occurs 328 times in the Bible.

A question often asked is, "Are all words of God directed for all people for all times?" The answer is clearly, "No." Often God spoke directly through a prophet to an individual, as in Exodus 4:22, 23: *Then you shall say to Pharaoh, "Thus says the Lord, "Israel is My son, My firstborn. So I said to you, 'Let My son go, that he may serve me'; but you have refused to let him go. Behold I will kill your son, your first-born."* Sometimes, he spoke to a specific group or church with revelation that was just for them in their time. An example is the letter to Philemon and the church that met in his house, telling them to receive back the runaway slave Onesimus. Principles from that short letter may apply to all people of all times, but the specific request was just for that church. Unfortunately, not everyone agrees on which directives were just for the immediate context and which are to be applied universally. For example, Paul told Timothy, who was probably the pastor of the church at Ephesus when he wrote that women should not braid their hair or wear gold, pearls, or expensive clothing (1 Timothy 2:9). He also instructed *men in every place to pray, lifting up holy hands* (1 Timothy 2:8). Cultural or universal commands?

In Scripture, we also see *Historic revelation* where God was speaking through the events of history. The struggles of Israel in Canaan provide examples of historic revelation. A valid question is whether events since the biblical days can also be considered to be historic revelation. Since history is his-story, presumably God continues to reveal himself through historic events. While much of prophecy has been fulfilled, God will continue to fulfill his plan through acts that may be considered to be historic revelation.

It's Alive!

One time I attended a training seminar sponsored by Inter-Varsity Fellowship. We were there to learn how to lead small group Bible studies. After we were seated in a circle, our teacher began the session by throwing her Bible on the floor in the middle of the group, jumping up on her chair and shrieking, "It's alive; it's alive!" Then, having captured our attention, she read the familiar words from Hebrews 4:12: *For the word of God is living and active.*

Maybe that's a bit too dramatic for some, but for over twenty years I have remembered that vivid demonstration of the vitality of Scripture.

If they come from God, surely the words we call Scripture are special. No other book or words can sway the destiny of people and nations like the Word(s) of God. No other book gives such a thorough understanding of God. No other book sets out the most superior way for humans to live. And no other book comes close to explaining the mystery of life.

But some might think it's just too good to be true, to think that the almighty, infinite, eternal God, the Sovereign of the universe, would personally oversee the writing of a collection of books for the human family. But there's another way of looking at this issue.

Imagine what it would be like to have a very powerful father who never spoke to you. You would never get to know him. You would never know what he did. You would never know what he liked or disliked. You would not be sure he loved you. You would only fear him and perhaps build up a severe case of insecurity.

What if that silent father was *Our Father in heaven*? We would be very frustrated, insecure, and fearful every day, not knowing how he felt about us, why he made us, or what he planned to do with us.

Well, thank God, he is not a silent God. He has spoken very clearly and completely, and his message is available to all of us. It is in a book, or rather, a library.

The Bible is an amazing collection of books that always have been recognized by God's people as accurate recordings of God's thoughts and activities regarding the human family. In this library are sixty-six "books" which present a wide variety of literature.

What kind of literature do you fancy – history? mysteries? romance? biography? adventure? drama? You will find them all in God's library. There are also books of poetry, narrative, philosophy, prophecy, and letters by famous Christians.

More than forty authors have contributed to this library over a period of about fifteen hundred years. But that is not what makes it so special. This library has been read by more people than any other series of books in all history, but still that is not what makes it so special. Hundreds of people have given their lives for this book, some of them being burned at the stake, yet that is not what makes it so special. Millions of people who have read these books have received guidance, comfort, and wisdom. More copies of this library are printed and sold every year than any other book[7], but that is not what makes it so special.

What makes the Bible so special is that in the truest sense, the publisher, editor, and author of this library of books is God himself! He did use human beings to write the books, but he is the Source of all that is in it! The books are, in the deepest sense, truly inspired.

Searching The Shelves

Let us explore how this library is structured. If it is truly a library, it ought to be orderly, and it is. There are two large sections—the Old Testament and the New Testament. The word *testament* means *covenant* or agreement. Both testaments tell how God chose to enter into relationships with people.

The old agreement had to do with a special race of people, the Jews, who were to be priests to the rest of the nations[8]. The sacrificial system was used to secure forgiveness of sins and allow people to know God.

The new agreement centers around a man, God's own Son in human flesh, who was sacrificed for the sins of the world. He has become our access to God. So, the basic theme of both testaments is the same: the story of how God has provided for sinful people to be forgiven and restored to a right relationship with himself. In a word, *redemption* is what the Bible is all about!

The "bookshelf" charts at the end of this chapter will help you see the orderly arrangement of the books of the Bible. The Old Testament shelves are in three sections: History, Prophecy, and Writings. The history and prophecy sections each have seventeen books and are subdivided into three sections: five major books (the Law and the Major Prophets), nine pre-exilic books and three post-exilic books.

This symmetry will help us remember where these books belong in the library. The first five books are called the Law, or the Pentateuch, meaning *five books*. The Hebrews called them the *Torah* and believed Moses was the author. They take us from the beginning of creation to the time when the large family of Israel came out of Egyptian bondage and were ready, after forty years of wandering, to go into the Promised Land.

The nine pre-exilic history books tell about the life of Israel up to BCE 586. That was the year when the

Babylonians destroyed Jerusalem, and the southern kingdom was carried off into exile. The ten northern tribes had already been deported in the eighth century BCE by the Assyrians. So the pre-exilic age was from Joshua to Jeremiah.

Then there are three books of post-exilic history; Ezra, Nehemiah, and Esther, which describe Israel's returning from exile and re-forming (but not reforming, unfortunately) as a nation.

After the seventeen historical books come the Writings, five books of poetry: Job, Psalms, Proverbs, Ecclesiastes, and Song of Solomon.

The third section has seventeen books of Prophecy, again divided into five, nine and three. The five are called Major Prophets, not because they are more important, but because they are longer. Then there are the Minor Prophets, nine that are pre-exilic, written before BCE 586, and three post-exilic. You now have an easy way to remember the books of the Old Testament!

17 History	5 Writings	17 Prophecy
5 Law		5 Major prophets
9 Pre-exile history		9 Minor Pre-exile prophets
3 Post-exile history		3 Minor Post-exile prophets

The "New" Shelves

The twenty-seven New Testament books are not called *new* just because they came later, but because they tell of a new or different agreement by which God relates to humans. There are two shelves which have three kinds of literature: History, Letters and Apocalyptic literature, a very special kind of writing.

Five books of history (paralleling the *Torah*) form the basic foundation of Christianity: the four Gospels and the Acts of the Apostles. The other twenty-two books divide into a nine—four—nine symmetry.

The Letters are nine church epistles written particularly with Gentiles in mind, all by the Apostle Paul. Then there are four personal letters by Paul, called the Pastoral Epistles. The last nine books are called the General Epistles, written by five or six different authors. These books are more concerned about the Jewish people and their response to Christianity.

The last book, *Revelation*, is the apocalyptic book. The Greek title is *Apocalypse,* meaning *revelation*. Apocalyptic literature was quite popular from BCE 200 to 200 CE. *Revelation* is typical of other such writings, very dramatic and filled with visions of the future. In fact, *Revelation* is a first century apocalyptic drama.[9] It differs from others apocalypses because it has apostolic authorship and inspirational status.

So, that is the Lord's library. Browse in it; read in it; study it; grow in it; live in it. God has spoken; let us not ignore him!

Looking Into The Canon

You might wonder, how do we know for sure there aren't other books in the Lord's library. Why do these sixty-six qualify, but others do not? Did God stop speaking? This is the question of canonicity. The canon is the whole body of biblical writings, and canonicity has to do with how it was determined which books were truly inspired.

The Bible did not just fall out of the sky with a glow on it and a note saying,

> *Dear people,*
> *This is for you, with all my love.*
> *Sincerely yours,*
> *God.*

We know that the books in the Bible were written by men who were aware of being inspired by God. Other men, however, wrote books and claimed them to be from God. Some early Christians thought other books should have been included in the Bible because they too were written by holy men. And some books that are in the Bible were challenged by people who thought they should not be included. The church faced the difficulty of deciding what should be considered a sacred writing.

This is also a modern question because many offshoots of biblical Christianity have been framed by earnest people who claim to have been inspired in their writing, or to have found sacred books or been given scrolls by an angel. They say these newer books have just as much authority as the books of the Bible. Canonicity is relevant and important.

Generally, the rule of thumb that was used by Jews to determine whether or not a book should be considered a sacred writing was its nearness in authorship to a true prophet. If a prophet or his scribe wrote it, its integrity was considered good. Some groups teach that the list of Old Testament books was finally agreed upon in 90 CE at the Jewish Council of Jamnia. Research shows that the rabbinic meeting in Jamnia was not a council, and concerned only the legitimacy of Ecclesiastes and Song of Solomon as part of the Scriptures. General consensus today is that the Old Testament scriptures were well agreed upon before the time of Christ.[10] One interesting note is the response of Jesus to the three temptations where three times he rebutted the tempter by saying, *The Scriptures say...*, implying that the Old Testament scriptures were already a canon. In fact, the word "Scriptures" occurs 28 times in the New Testament, most often used by Jesus.

The New Testament books had to be related closely to an apostle. For example, of our four gospels, only two were written by apostles, Matthew and John. Mark, however, was the companion and probably a companion of Peter, who was Mark's primary source of information.

Luke was Paul's companion, and a firsthand observer of many of the events recorded in Acts. Luke even gives his credentials for writing at the beginning of his Gospel and Acts:

> *In as much as many have undertaken to compile an account of the things accomplished among us, just as they were handed down to us by those who from the beginning were eyewitnesses and servants of the word, it seemed fitting for me as well, having investigated everything carefully from the beginning, to write it out for you in consecutive order, most excellent Theophilus; so that you may know the*

> *exact truth about the things you have been*
> *taught* (Luke 1:1-4).

Luke as author engaged in detailed, investigative, historical work, going right to the eyewitness sources of his information. As a highly-educated Gentile, he was not about to accept blindly the claims of a Jewish messianic figure. No doubt Paul's influence on him as a writer was great.

The debate over some New Testament books continued for several centuries. The New Testament canon was ratified in 363 CE by the Council of Laodicea.

Since the biblical books needed prophetic or apostolic endorsement, the issue of canonicity is really a historical one. We cannot go back nineteen hundred years or more to reevaluate whether or not various books should be included. Nor from our historical vantage point can we decide to veto the decisions made then. It is not our prerogative to add or delete any of the books or any portions of them. Those who made the decisions hundreds of years ago were far more qualified than anyone alive today, if only because of their historical advantage; they lived closer to the events described in the Bible.

As an illustration of this, suppose as a reporter you are required to write a report about the emotional trauma of children who lived in London during the bombings of World War II. Thousands of books have been written about that war, some by people who lived through it, others by people who have just studied it. Which books would be more valuable to you? Obviously, those written by people who were children who lived in London during the actual bombings would be most valuable. The closer you can get to the events themselves, the more reliable your report will be. That is why we accept as sacred those books agreed upon by the early Jewish and Christian communities.

Here, then, is the list of Sacred Books, those chosen to be considered to be the Word of God by the people of God throughout history.

Old Testament Chart

Old Testament—39 Books

HISTORY—17 Books	PROPHECY—17 Books
Law	**Major Prophets**
Genesis—*beginnings*	Isaiah—*evangelical*
Exodus—*deliverance*	Jeremiah—*doom*
Leviticus—*laws*	Lamentations—*weeping*
Numbers—*wanderings*	Ezekiel—*visions*
Deuteronomy—*review*	Daniel—*prediction*
Pre-exilic	**Pre-exilic**
Joshua—*conquest*	Hosea—*fidelity*
Judges—*confusion*	Joel—*locust plague*
Ruth—*lineage*	Amos—*justice*
1 Samuel—*Saul*	Obadiah—*Edom*
2 Samuel—*David*	Jonah—*Nineveh*
1 Kings—*division*	Micah—*social*
2 Kings—*defeat*	Nahum—*Nineveh*
1 Chronicles—*David*	Habakkuk—*prophet's protest*
2 Chronicles—*kings of Judah*	Zephaniah—*day of the Lord*
Post-exilic	**Post-exilic**
Ezra—*rebuilding temple*	Haggai—*restore temple*
Nehemiah—*rebuilding wall*	Zechariah—*apocalyptic*
Esther—*Hebrews preserved*	Malachi—*obedience*

POETRY—5 Books
Job—*testing*
Psalms—*song book*
Proverbs—*wisdom*
Ecclesiastes—*vanity*
Song of Solomon—*love song*

New Testament Chart

New Testament—27 Books

HISTORY
Gospels
  Matthew—*kingdom*
  Mark—*Servant*
  Luke—*Son of man*
  John—*Son of God*
Acts—*church progress*
CHURCH EPISTLES—Gentile
Romans—*justification*
1 Corinthians—*discipline*
2 Corinthians—*discipline*
Galatians—*legalism*
Ephesians—*doctrine*
Philippians—*joy*
Colossians—*world view*
1 Thessalonians—*Second Coming*
2 Thessalonians—*Second Coming*

PASTORAL EPISTLES

1 Timothy—*pastoral*
2 Timothy—*pastoral*
Titus—*pastoral*
Philemon—*runaway*

HEBREW CHRISTIAN EPISTLES
Hebrews—*types*
James—*works*
1 Peter—*hope*
2 Peter—*hope*
1 John—*love*
2 John—*love*
3 John—*love*
Jude—*apostasy*
Revelation—*apocalypse*

Chapter 7

Truly Inspired

Because the information recorded in the Bible is so foundational to our faith, we naturally want to know how we got the Bible and whether we can fully trust it. The Bible did not come just floating down out of the sky in black leather binding, fresh from the printing press of heaven. Even though it is God's book, humans had a major role in writing and preserving it.

None of the original manuscripts of the Bible exist today. Presumably, they are all lost, destroyed or decomposed. There are in existence, however, thousands of manuscripts that were based on the originals, or very ancient copies. Some of the New Testament manuscripts date back as far as 400 CE. I have seen two of the three most valuable New Testament manuscripts at the British Museum in London. It is an awesome thought to realize you are looking at books written a few generations after Jesus lived on earth.

Until 1947, the earliest Old Testament manuscripts available were written in about 1000 CE. That is a long time away from the actual events. But in 1947, the Dead Sea Scrolls were discovered in caves in the Dead Sea area of Israel. Some 600 fragments and scrolls were found in pottery jars, so we now have manuscripts of all or parts of every Old Testament book except Esther, and some of them date back to the second century BCE. These scrolls were probably copied by scribes of the Essene community of Jews who hid them during a time of war. This amazing discovery has cleared up many textual questions about the Old Testament, but more significantly it has shown us the remarkable accuracy of the much later manuscripts.

Ghost Writer

The other answer to the question, "How did we get the Bible?" focuses on the activity of God in providing us with the information. God himself has told us how he worked with the human writers to give us his Word. Second Peter 1:21 tells us: *For no prophecy was ever made by an act of human will but men moved by the Holy Spirit spoke from God.*

Paul mentions a similar fact, applying it to all Scripture; *All Scripture is inspired by God and profitable for teaching, for reproof, for correction, for training in righteousness;* (2 Timothy 3:16). The word *inspiration* is often used to express how the Bible is unique as a book. Literally, it means God-breathed. God has breathed his Word through the various human writers. We may say with reverence that he is the ghost writer. A ghost writer is someone who writes a book for someone else whose name appears as the author. The Holy Spirit (or Holy Ghost) is the author who wrote through Moses, David, Isaiah, John, Paul, and the others.

There are several theories of inspiration that emphasize different relationships between God and the human writers. These are worth considering because the issue of inspiration is so important to our Christian lives. Ultimately what we believe about God, what we know about Jesus, and how we respond to God depend on the reliability of the Bible. Its degree of trustworthiness would not be great if it is just a collection of myths, fables, poetry, and human opinions.

On the other hand, if it does, in fact, reflect the mind of God, it is certainly worthy of our full confidence. The diagram below shows how five theories of inspiration relate to the activity of man in producing the scriptures:

God's Part				Man's Part
Mechanical	Dictational	Dynamic	Illumination	Natural Intuition

The mechanical view sees the human writers as totally passive to the dominance of God; they are merely human typewriters and God punches the keys. They have nothing to do with the end product, nor does it reflect their personality or perspective. The key word here is *passive*. Few people hold to this point of view, as it seems that the writers were always at least conscious and actively responsive to God's Spirit as they wrote.

The dictational view also stresses the control of God, but allows for the human writer to be consciously involved. Just like a secretary writes down the exact words the boss dictates for a report or a letter, so the biblical writers were totally submissive to God's dictation of the exact words he gave to them. The key word here is *submissive*. This differs from the mechanical view just as a secretary taking dictation differs from a typewriter. The secretary is consciously involved in the process and must use certain human skills and aptitude to do it. But the end product reflects neither the ideas nor the vocabulary of the human writer, but of God. In other words, in the dictational view the writers of Scripture were acting as scribes, not as authors. We get the sense that God used this type of inspiration to give the Ten Commandments to Moses and a few other places in Scripture.

The dynamic view emphasizes a balanced involvement between the Spirit of God and the intelligence, experiences, and personality of the human writer. A certain dynamic between the two beings both involved in the tasks resulted in the finished product. God inspired the information and the writer expressed it through his personality, his world perspective, and his vocabulary. Using a business analogy, God as the publisher tells the writer what he wants in the book, gives him divine insight and enabling, but reserves editorial privileges so that the finished book reflects both the intelligence and personality of the writer, but also the perspective and authority of God, the publisher and editor. In this sense, the dynamic view sees the writing of Scripture as a *cooperative* effort.

The illumination view argues that while God gave the basic ideas or concepts to the writers, the Scriptures are highly colored by each author's personality, creativity, insight, and verbal expression. They wrote as men *enlightened* by God and responsive to him but having considerable freedom of expression. In this view, God inspired the concepts but not the specific words themselves. The author used his own vocabulary, sentence structure, idioms, and language style to communicate God's message. He also wrote out of his own historical background and cultural orientation. This type of authorship is like a man who researches a primary document of someone else who is very knowledgeable, and then reports on it in his own terms. He is the author, but he is greatly influenced and enlightened by a greater authority.

The natural intuition view is the fifth theory, and it emphasizes little control by God and great control by the human authors. The writers, in this view, were godly people but their writing was *verbally independent* of any direct control by God. This is similar to the kind of inspiration recognized in great poets like Shakespeare and Milton, who were "inspired" by concepts and creative minds. Their works, however, are not supernatural; they are just extraordinary. In this theory, God's responsibility for Scripture lies only in the fact that he is the ultimate Source of all life and intelligence, and brought these particularly gifted and holy writers to the world at strategic times in his own plan.

So What?

Perhaps this discussion of inspiration seems a bit abstract and irrelevant. Your response may be, "So what? What's this got to do with being a Christian?" Simply this: if you ever tell others about your Christian convictions, you will likely be challenged about why you believe the Bible is God's Word. How do you know it is true? Why do you put your trust in what it says? Suppose you are witnessing to someone and start to say, "Well, the Bible says...," and then you get cut off by the person saying, "I don't care what the Bible says; I don't believe in it. Why should I?"

What are going to say? "Well, it is real old, and they tell us at church that it is really God's Word."

Not quite! Your friend would come back with, "But why do you believe it?"

Maybe then you would say, "Because it is inspired by God."

"Well, what in the world does that mean? Did God shout out of the clouds in Hebrew?"

This discussion on inspiration will help you to be able to respond to that kind of challenge.

Which Is Right?

To arrive at a realistic appraisal of how the Bible was inspired we might begin by crossing off the two extreme views. The mechanical view is inadequate because the holy writers were always conscious of what they were writing even though they may not have always fully understood it. The natural intuition view nearly excludes God and contradicts the meaning of *inspiration—God-breathed.*

The dictational method was used at times, no doubt. For example: *In the fourth year of Jehoiakim the son of Josiah, king of Judah, this word came to Jeremiah from the Lord, saying, "Take a scroll and write on it all the words which I have spoken to you concerning Israel and concerning Judah, and concerning all the nations, from the day I first spoke to you, from the days of Josiah, even to this day* (Jeremiah 36:1-2).

It is not likely, however, that dictation was the primary method God used to inspire the writing of most Scripture. More frequently the dynamic method was used, where God superintended and inspired it verbally.

Here we need to make a distinction. An ongoing debate focuses on the difference between verbal inspiration and conceptual inspiration. Perhaps this is the key difference between the dynamic and the illumination theories. Verbal inspiration means that God told the writers what to say and what words to use. Conceptual inspiration suggests that God gave the basic ideas and the authors used their own vocabulary to express those ideas.

For example, a teacher may ask a student to bring to the class a report about the book *War and Peace*. The teacher may also say, "I want you to discuss when it was written, why it was written, and who wrote it." It would then be the student's job to do the studying and use his or her own words to communicate the ideas. That would be like conceptual inspiration. Or, the teacher may say, "In the *Introduction* the author tells why he wrote the book; learn this by heart and present it to us." That would be more like verbal inspiration.

Personally, I believe most of the Bible was verbally inspired, so I would opt for the dynamic view to be my prevailing theory of inspiration. There may not be a thick wall separating this view from the illumination theory, but I do not believe that the Bible is only conceptually inspired. One reason I believe this is that considering the nature of God, who spared no detail in arranging the earth which is disposable, and considering the high stakes of the message of the Bible, it seems reasonable that God would care very much about precision and accuracy of expression in communicating eternal truth.

We must admit, however, that the vocabulary and language style of the various writers of Scripture vary tremendously. Those who know New Testament Greek will tell you that John's writing is very basic, elementary Greek, perhaps third-grade level. Paul's writing is a bit more complex and shows a larger vocabulary, perhaps high school level. When you turn to Luke or Hebrews, unless you know Greek very well, you may as well be trying to read Urdu. Those authors wrote with a very polished, sophisticated style and vocabulary – Ph. D. level. But this difference of vocabulary and language style does not rule out the idea of verbal inspiration. Rather, it emphasizes God's versatility, which fits neatly within his sovereignty and his purpose for each book and its intended first audience.

What's The Word?

One other aspect of inspiration needs to be considered – the extent of, or more accurately the location of, the inspiration. To avoid making any supernatural claims about a book, sometimes people in our day get a bit tricky and say that the Bible merely contains the Word of God or becomes the Word of God. A Scripture often given falsely as proof of this idea is 2 Corinthians 3:6, ...*the letter kills, but the Spirit gives life.* The interpretation given, then, is that the words themselves are dead and of no great value unless and until the Spirit speaks them into my life situation or blesses me through them. Others may say that in the Word I may encounter Christ, but unless that happens, it is not the Word.

Now, this may sound very spiritual and may seem to explain why sometimes when I read Scripture I do not "get anything out of it," but it is wrong. The Bible is the Word of God regardless of how I perceive it or respond to it! Fire is still fire whether or not I stick my hand in it and get burned. God has spoken, it has been recorded, and the result is his Word, totally and always. Scripture does not *contain* or *become* the Word of God. It *is* the Word of God!

But Can I Trust It?

So, we have very old texts, which ancient people agreed were supernaturally inspired. Fine, but can I trust it today? Many people do not accept the Bible as God's Word, and some even make fun of it and anyone who believes it. Claims about contradictions, historical error, impossible historical events, scientific error, and other problems are cited with a skeptical assurance that truly the Bible is unreliable, merely an ancient record, now known to be faulty.

While this is probably the most complicated topic we could explore, one thing is certain: the area of controversy may be shrunken down to a much smaller field than is generally thought. For instance, it is often alleged that the Bible and science are not compatible. So, many people write off the Bible as fiction or faulty history in favor of the inerrancy of science. While it is true that the Bible does not purport to be a science textbook, the discussion should really be about what the Bible actually says (not imposed interpretations) and what science has actually proven to be true (not mere theories).[11]

A word that expresses the reliability and trustworthiness of the Bible is *inerrancy,* which means totally free from error. When we talk about the Bible being inerrant, we refer to the belief that the books of Scripture were without error in the original writing. No one believes in the inerrancy of the later manuscripts because the copyists were not inspired and copy errors did occur. Punctuation, misspelling, and omissions plagued ancient scribes as much as they do modern school children or typists. Comparing the thousands of extant copies, however, allows us to "weed out" the errors and produce a nearly perfect text.

Inerrancy refers to the belief that the original manuscripts were 100 percent correct. Admittedly, this is an assumption because we do not have any of the original manuscripts to check out. It is, however, a position of faith and it is reasonable because of the nature of inspiration. Since God is perfect, holy, and flawless, God-breathed books also would be errorless.

Section Two:
The Son and the Gospel

Chapter 8

The Heaven-Sent Son

The Bible is not a collection of stories – neither is it just a history book. It follows the great theme of how men and women can come into a right relationship with God. The entire Old Testament points toward one thing – God's provision for making people right with himself through his son, Jesus Christ.

Think of history by using this diagram.

Creation	Call to Abraham	Moses and Lamb Sacrifice	David and Kingly Line	Incarnation of Jesus	Death, Resurrection, Ascension	Second Coming of Jesus
	1900 B.C.	1300 B.C.	1000 B.C.	4 B.C.	A.D. 30	?

Even at the beginning, there were hints that God would do something meaningful and special in history. In order to achieve his purpose of saving people from the consequences of sin, God began to work with a remnant of society that came from the family of Abraham. Their one mission was to be faithful to God until he would send the Messiah or Savior through them. To help them repent of their sins and trust him for righteousness, God instituted the sacrificial system in the days of Moses. Blood sacrifices of animals were used to show how serious God takes sin. He also told Israel that the Messiah would come through the royal family of King David, and he would be the final blood sacrifice. See Luke 24:25-27.

When the Messiah did come, all history focused on the cross, but not everyone knew how significant it was that Jesus had died. The crucifixion was not a publicly newsworthy event that made the headlines of the *Jerusalem Journal* or the *Rome Daily Rag,* but from God's point of view all history pivoted on the cross. Now history is continuing toward a climactic end when Jesus will return. It is most appropriate, therefore, that we carefully consider Jesus Christ. We will not be emphasizing the stories particularly, since they are fairly well known by most Christians. We will be somewhat philosophical or theological, considering why he came, what his real nature was, what his teachings were, and what we are to expect of him.

Life Before Birth

One of the questions that concerns everyone is, "Is there life after death?" We will look into that later. We never, however, consider the possibility of life before birth, which was exactly the experience of Jesus Christ. He actually lived before he was born or conceived. No one else in history can make that claim. Theologians call this the preexistence of Jesus, which is a well-documented fact in Scripture. Although he came to earth as a baby, Jesus had already lived in eternity as the Son of God.

The Bible tells us several facts about his preexistence. Jesus once confounded his critics this way: *Your father Abraham rejoiced to see My day, and he saw it and was glad. So the Jews said to Him, "You are not yet fifty years old, and have You seen Abraham?" Jesus said to them, "Truly, truly, I say to you, before Abraham was born, I am"* (John 8:56-58).

The preexistence of Jesus, however, refers not only to his existence in the days of the patriarchs, but also to being with the Father before the world was created. In his "high priestly" prayer, Jesus said, *I glorified You on the earth, having accomplished the work which You have given Me to do. Now, Father, glorify Me together with Yourself, with the glory which I had with You before the world was* (John 17:4, 5*)*.

Not only was he there before creation, he was also very active in the work of creation. If someone were to ask you who the Creator is, and your answer, "God," meaning the Father, you would not be entirely correct. Two Scriptures affirm that God the Son was also actively involved. Speaking of Jesus, Paul wrote, ... *by Him all things were created, both in the heavens and on earth, visible and invisible, whether thrones or dominions or rulers or authorities-- all things have been created by Him and for Him* (Colossians 1:16). Hebrews 1:2 says *whom* (Christ) *He* (God) *made the world*. So, you can see, Christ was quite busy before he was born!

It Appears He Appeared

Jesus may also have appeared on earth in Old Testament days. Joshua 5:13-15 gives one instance: *Now it came about when Joshua was by Jericho, that he lifted up his eyes and looked, and behold, a man was standing opposite him with his sword drawn in his hand, and Joshua went to him and said to him, "Are you for us or for our adversaries?" He said, "No; rather I indeed come now as captain of the host of the Lord." And Joshua fell on his face to the earth, and bowed down, and said to him, "What has my lord to say to his servant?" The captain of the Lord's host said to Joshua, "Remove your sandals from your feet, for the place where you are standing is holy." And Joshua did so.*

Some scholars believe this commander of the Lord's army was the pre-existent form of our Lord Jesus making an Old Testament appearance. No other being, including angels, would have received Joshua's worship. Several times when angels appeared to a man, he would bow to worship, but the angels always forbad it. See, for example, Revelation 22:8, 9.

Daniel gave the account of the three children of Israel, Shadrach, Meshach, and Abednego, who were thrown into the fiery furnace because they refused to bow to the idol of Babylonian King Nebuchadnezzar. With them appeared in the furnace a fourth person whom Nebuchadnezzar said "*looks like a son of the gods.*" It was likely the Son of God who protected the three from being burned.

Genesis 32 tells about Jacob wrestling with a "man," whom he later discovered was an appearance of God. Several times Old Testament people assumed an angel had appeared to them, but a careful look at the incidents leads us to believe that Christ made many other Old Testament appearances. Here are other Scriptures that tell of such visitations, known as *Christophanies* or manifestations of Christ:

Genesis 18:1-8 (to Abraham)
Exodus 3:1-11 (to Moses)
Judges 2:1-5 (to Israel)
Judges 6:11-24 (to Gideon)
Judges 13:2-25 (to Manoah)

The First Word

John's Gospel begins: *In the beginning was the Word, and the Word was with God, and the Word was God. He was in the beginning with God* (John 1:1,2). What did John mean by this Word? What Word did John have in mind? He did not mean a noun or verb or adjective that you would find in the dictionary because he called that *Word* "he." When we talk about the Word of God, we do not always mean the printed Word, the Bible. Sometimes we use that title for Jesus, to whom John was referring.

A well-loved hymn begins, "O Word of God incarnate." The word *incarnate* means "in the flesh." Jesus was the full expression of God in flesh. In Greek culture in the days of Jesus, the word *Word (Logos)* referred to the one thing that made everything else make sense, the one expression that defined everything else. John's Gospel says that Jesus is that One who makes sense out of all the questions and mysteries of the world. He does so because as the pre-existent Son of God, he has always lived. Certainly, it is a mysterious concept that one could live before his birth, but when that one is part of the Godhead, it makes sense.

Why He Came

More amazing than his pre-existence, however, is the fact that Jesus would reduce himself to human form. He must have had good reasons. We will consider five biblical reasons for Jesus coming to earth. The first one is found in the Christmas story. The angel announced to Joseph, ...*you shall call His name Jesus, for it is He who will save His people from their sins* (Matthew 1:21). He came primarily to save people from sins.

The second reason tells how he did that. He came to be the sacrifice demanded as the price for sin, or to use another good biblical word, he came as a ransom. In Matthew 20:28 Jesus, talking about himself said, ...*the Son of Man did not come to be served, but to serve, and to give His life as a ransom for many.*

One time Jesus was with a group of sinners, which made the religious leaders intensely critical. His reply to them was, *It is not those who are healthy who need a physician, but those who are sick...I did not come to call the righteous, but sinners* (Matthew 9:12-13). He was talking about people who are spiritually sick.

The truth is, all of us are spiritually sick and need the ministry of Jesus, the spiritual doctor, but some people will not admit their need. Such people, like the self-righteous Pharisees, will never enjoy the third purpose for which Jesus came.

Third, Jesus came to give *abundant life* (John 10:10). What did he mean by abundant life? It is the kind of life in which believers are fully alive to all God created us for. Most people walking around today, however, are spiritually dead. They do not know God and have not asked to be made spiritually alive. They cannot talk with God, even if they think they can, because it is through the Spirit that we communicate with God.

Now, most people enjoy life physically (beautiful flowers, tasty food, and good music), and socially (parties, sports, fun, and vacations) because they are alive physically and socially. But they do not have abundant life because they are missing out on an entire area of life, the spiritual. They cannot even begin to understand that area because it seems unreal to them.

Imagine trying to describe the color green to a person who always has been blind – impossible! That person would not have the capacity to experience or even to understand the concept of colors. So it is with people who are not spiritually alive; they cannot possibly experience abundant life, which includes knowing God personally.

Fourth, Jesus came to earth to provide eternal life, which is abundant life forever. *For God so loved the world, that He gave His only begotten Son, that whoever believes in Him should not perish, but have eternal life* (John 3:16).

We know this verse so well that we seldom think about its meaning when we read it or recite it. God wants people to live forever with himself; He does not want anyone to perish. Eternal life means the kind of life God has, not bound by space or time limitations. Abundant life forever—make sure you do not miss out on it. What is more important than that? *For what will a man be profited, if he gains the whole world, and forfeits his soul? Or what will a man give in exchange for his soul?* (Matthew 16:26).

Fifth, Jesus came to show us what God is like. Jesus is the closest thing we have to a picture of God. Of course, we are not thinking about a physical photo, for God is spirit. In terms of God's character, though, if you want to know what God is like, look at Jesus. How does God respond to people? Look at Jesus. What is God most concerned about? Look at Jesus. What does God want to do in the lives of people? Look at Jesus. John 1:18 tells us, *No man has seen God at any time; the only begotten God, who is in the bosom of the Father, He has explained Him.* That is, Jesus has given us a true picture of the nature of God.

All God; All Man

Normally, one plus one equals two, but not in the case of Jesus. As we saw in chapter 5, the Bible indicates that Jesus is fully God and fully man at the same time. Mathematically, he would have to be two people or one-half man and one-half God. But neither of these is the case. He is one person, even though he is fully God and fully man. That, admittedly, is quite a mystery which we will explore now. We begin with a spirit of humility, acknowledging that our minds cannot understand the mysteries of God. We will never fully understand God. The dual nature of Jesus is so incomprehensible that no human analogy can help us. Actually, we can best talk about the nature of Jesus by saying what he is not.

Scripture gives no evidence of a dual personality in Jesus. He was not, in modern psychological language, schizophrenic. He was the essence of consistency and wholeness. Jesus never spoke of himself in the plural; rather, he seemed to be always conscious of his full identity with man and of his unique relationship with God the Father and the Holy Spirit.

The Bible always represents both natures – human and divine – as united in one person. In Romans 1:3-4 Paul wrote about God's gospel,…*concerning His Son, who born of a descendant of David according to the flesh, who was declared the Son of God with power.* This dual nature is seen also in Galatians 4:4, 5: *But when the fullness of time came, God sent forth His Son, born of a woman, born under the Law, in order that He might redeem those who were under the Law.* Both natures are represented as being in one person.

Scripture teaches that the eternal Son of God took upon himself our humanity, and not that the man Jesus acquired a divine nature. *Who, although He existed in the form of God, did not regard equality with God a thing to be grasped, but emptied Himself, taking the form of a bond-servant, and being made in the likeness of men* (Philippians 2:6,7).

Some people have said that Jesus was really God who came to earth but remained totally divine without sharing our humanity, except in physical appearance. Others have said that Jesus never was God; he was only a man in whom God dwelt in a special way. Both of these concepts are wrong. Jesus came as fully man and fully God. He was one being totally divine and totally human.[12]

This twofold nature in one person does not register as reasonable to our minds because it is not part of our experience and because it seems rationally impossible. It is a mystery before which we must bow and admit our own finiteness. God does not need our permission to act in ways that transcend our understanding. He does not submit or reduce his will to human intelligence for acceptance or approval; rather, he insists that we submit our minds to his will. The reason people do not accept biblical doctrines is that their minds are their god, the final judge of truth. It is far better to submit humbly to the mystery of the Godhead and appreciate both the full humanity and full divinity of Jesus.

Chapter 9

What's the Good News?

The word *gospel* means "good news," but it is a particular kind of good news. More than just the ordinary good news that your favorite ball team won a game or your boss gave you a raise, this good news is about something God has done for all people. The good news is that Jesus Christ came into the world to give his life to save sinners from eternal punishment.

When Mark began his Gospel, which was quite likely the first Gospel to have been written, he started by saying, *The beginning of the gospel of Jesus Christ, the Son of God.* When did it begin? It actually began before his birth.

In Matthew and Luke, we have the story of an angel coming to make an announcement of the beginning of the Good News. A baby would be born, and as he would grow, it would be obvious that he was an exceptional person.

As Jesus began his life's work, he did things that the Old Testament predicted would be done by the Messiah, God's chosen one. He opened the eyes of people who had been blind all their lives. He healed the withered hand of a man in the synagogue. He healed someone who had never walked a step all his life so that he could walk perfectly.

A woman suffering from a disease for twelve years touched his robe and was healed. In the home of a synagogue official whose little daughter had just died, he simply said, *Little girl, I say to you, get up!* and she came back to life. He did many outstanding acts like this, not just for the people involved, but as a sign to all the Jews. It was God's way of saying that in the person of Jesus, God was present in a very unusual and new way.

Messiah's Message

The Old Testament had foretold this. *The Spirit of the Lord God is upon me, because the Lord has anointed me to bring good news to the afflicted. He has sent me to bind up the brokenhearted, to proclaim liberty to captives, and freedom to prisoners* (Isaiah 61:1). When these old predictions finally started happening, that was really good news.

In Matthew's Gospel, there is much teaching about a kingdom. Israel had been told in Exodus 19:4-6 that God wanted her to be a kingdom of priests and a holy nation. When Jesus came to begin his kingdom, he included Jews and Gentiles. Anyone can be in that kingdom. God's people, the community of believers all over the world, are members of the kingdom of God. The good news of the gospel is that the kingdom has begun. We do not need to wait until we die and go to heaven to begin to participate in the kingdom of God. It is already here. That is good news!

One sent from God with such a unique role, who retained his full divinity as he took on full humanity, obviously had something important to say. Jesus came as Messiah, the "Anointed One." An anointing was usually done upon someone who would become king, and so it was with Jesus. He was Messiah; he was King; but mostly he was called Rabbi, meaning teacher. Some people thought he was only a teacher, rejecting the possibility of his being Messiah and King. Others said he was a prophet. The disciples came to the conclusion that he was the Son of God. Actually, he was all these things—Messiah, King, Teacher, Prophet, and Son of God—so obviously, what he said must have been most important.

The main theme of his teaching was about the kingdom of God, which he said was not like other political empires like the Assyrians, Babylonians, Persians, Greeks, and Romans. Instead, the kingdom of God exists side by side with political empires, flowing through the lives of many people. When most of us think about the kingdom of God, we think about heaven. But the kingdom of God is more than that. In heaven, God's kingdom will be untainted by the presence of sin, but on earth God's reign is visible only in the lives of those who live under the kingship of Jesus Christ.

Kingdom Citizenship

Most important for us, however, is not where the kingdom is or what it is like, but how we get into the kingdom. There are probably many people who know much about the kingdom of God but have never become citizens of it, just as one might know much about China without having been there.

Jesus responded in three ways to the question of entrance into God's kingdom. The three answers are basically the same but present different ways of looking at the issue. To Nicodemus, who was an intelligent Jewish leader and probably a devout man, Jesus said, *Truly, truly, I say to you, unless one is born again he cannot see the kingdom of God...I say to you, unless one is born of water and the Spirit, he cannot enter into the kingdom of God (John 3:3,5).* The first and most fundamental entrance requirement is being born again.

The second statement has to do with repentance, which is part of becoming born again. When Jesus began his preaching ministry, his message was summed up in one sentence, *Repent, for the kingdom of heaven is at hand* (Matthew 4:17). Repentance involves our intellect, emotions, and will. With our mind we understand how we have violated God's will and sinned; with our emotions we sorrow over our rebelliousness and ingratitude, and with our will we do a complete turnabout in the way we live. People who do not repent deeply lack an understanding of both the holiness of God and the offensiveness to God of their own sinful nature. All citizens of God's kingdom have repented of their sins.

Third, to be citizens of God's kingdom we must have no higher allegiance; that is, our heart must be set on living for that kingdom. We must *seek first His kingdom and His righteousness* (Matthew 6:33). In Matthew 19 a rich young ruler asked Jesus how to get into the kingdom. The young man seemed like a good prospect because he said he had kept the commandments Jesus mentioned. But Jesus, seeing that the man lived for his riches, told him to sell his possessions and give to the poor. The young man could not do it; his property owned him! That is why Jesus said: *it is easier for a camel to go through the eye of a needle, than for rich man to enter the kingdom of God* (Matthew 19:24). Whatever we put before God's kingdom will keep us out of it.

Live And Learn

As a great teacher, Jesus spoke about many other themes, but he differed from other teachers in that he did not expect his followers to acquire much head knowledge so that they could then live better. Rather, he knew that once they had become members of the kingdom of God, they would have inner power to live the lessons he was teaching them. He told His followers that inner power would come from the Spirit of Truth who will *teach you all things and bring to your remembrance all that I have said to you* (John 14:26). All the parables, beatitudes, warnings, promises, proverbs, and doctrines that were part of his teaching are important for us to know. Being a member of His kingdom, however, is more important so that we will not only know his teaching but also will live it.

Old News That's New

For most people today, the story of Jesus is not really fresh news. It is not the kind of hot news item that you might hear in the street, "Get your paper! Son of God has come to save sinners?" But if that happened and someone replied, "Oh, yeah? Really? When did that happen?"

"Well, about two thousand years ago…."

It is really not news in that sense anymore.

In the first century, however, it was big news that this One who had been promised, first to Abraham and to the other patriarchs; to David and to the children of Israel; and then by the prophets to the whole world, was now actually present. It had happened; he had come into the world. It was good, fresh news.

For many people today, however, it is old news and they are not particularly excited about it. You might have grown up hearing the gospel over and over again. It is not fresh news for you and maybe you are not sure that it is good news at all because of the standards it sets for your life. How then is it good news?

Amazing Grace

The good news of God contrasts sharply with some bad news. The bad news is that we who were created in God's image chose, in Adam and Eve, to rebel against him and his standards. You might think that it is unfair of God to penalize us for a sin committed by the first humans. It is true that we inherited our sinful tendencies from them, but any honest person knows we have all sinned and rebelled against God's holy standards.

Conceivably, after the first humans became sinners, God could have crumpled up the earth in his hands and thrown it into the trash can of the universe and be done with this rebellious planet and people. Why, then, did

God bring salvation to this earth instead? God wanted to fulfill his original purpose of being a Father to a family, and loving us, he wanted to meet our need. We should get that clearly in our understanding. God *wanted* to meet our need but *was not required* to do so.

We may think that God was obligated to send Jesus into the world to forgive us. He was not. God does not owe us a thing. God could have justly condemned all people because we are all rebels and enemies of God. He did not have to do one thing for us.

We emphasize this because one thing that is greatly lacking in Christians today is the sense of deep gratitude to God. Sometimes we act toward God as though he owes us everything. He does not owe us anything. His provision of salvation is the result of what the Bible calls grace. The basic meaning of the word *grace* is good will or generous spirit. Grace is the unmerited favor God bestows on us.

Interestingly, the Greek word for *grace* is related to the words *joy* and *gift*. Salvation is God's gift, his gracious gift to us for our joy. He did not owe it to us.

Another definition of the word *grace* is the inclination of God to be kindly disposed to all people. That is why God brought salvation to the world – He has that kindly inclination. That is truly good news.

Dynamite That Saves

In Romans 1:16 Paul said that he was not *ashamed of the gospel* because in it God has revealed a particular type of power, *the power of God for salvation to everyone who believes*. The Greek word for *power* sounds like "dynamite." Without the gospel, the good news of the life of Jesus, God had no other way of saving sinners. It is God's only means of reaching people who are away from him in sin. In other words, if there were no gospel, we would still be apart from God, guilty, and condemned. The gospel is good news about how we can be saved. It is God's dynamite.

The Bigness Of Salvation

When we think of *salvation,* we are using a word with which we are familiar but an idea that is much bigger than we think. What is meant by salvation? When did your salvation really start? When you became a Christian? Maybe it started even earlier than that.

Your salvation actually began when God chose you before the creation of the world. *Blessed be the God and Father of our Lord Jesus Christ, who has blessed us with every spiritual blessing in the heavenly places in Christ, just as He chose us in Him before the foundation of the world, that we would be holy and blameless before Him. In love He predestined us to adoption as sons through Jesus Christ to Himself, according to the kind intention of His will* (Ephesians 1:3-5). Your salvation did not begin when you first heard the gospel, nor even when you were born; it began before that. This is called the doctrine of *election,* God's choosing you for salvation.

Another part of salvation is *justification,* which is God's declaring you legally righteous. Before becoming a Christian you were a spiritual criminal, guilty before God of sinning, but God had already done something about that. He had already paid the price and declared you legally righteous.

Reconciliation, also part of salvation, means the making of friends of those who were enemies. In Scripture, the idea is that we are enemies of God until he reconciles us to himself, and we become his friends. That is part of salvation.

Another part of salvation, *regeneration,* means to make something come alive. Our spirits are regenerated when we are born again.

Sanctification is another part of salvation. It means *set apart for a holy purpose.* Christians are set apart for a holy purpose. Christians are set apart by God for righteous purposes. Sanctification is the growth process of maturing spiritually. Often, it begins with a crisis experience and then becomes a daily progression of living in obedience to God.

Healing is also available through our salvation. Even though many Christians do not believe it or appropriate it, God still heals people in our day from infirmities, sicknesses, and diseases. When he died on the cross, Jesus Christ made provision for our physical restoration as well as our spiritual life.

The last part of salvation is *glorification.* When we enter the presence of God with our new bodies and are glorified with Christ, that will be the final aspect of salvation.

So, salvation started when we were chosen before the creation of the world. When will it conclude? Never. The final aspect of salvation is our glorification when we see the Lord and become like him. This will last for all eternity.

If that isn't good news, then I have never heard any.

Chapter 10

Jesus on Trial

The gospel we have been considering is good news about a person, Jesus Christ. The claim is made that in that one person, all meaning in life and the hereafter is to be found. Now, that's a rather preposterous claim. If it is true, of course, it is good news; in fact, great news! But it all hangs on the truthfulness of the claim about Jesus Christ. An issue of such great weight needs to be thoroughly investigated and considered. Our best effort is called for. You will not want to put your eternal destiny, or even your investment of this life, in a claim that you haven't substantiated to your own satisfaction.

So, let us convene as a jury to judge the claims made about Jesus. There are two specific and rather sensational claims about him that need to be considered. The first one has to do with his identity; the second, with his destiny.

True Christians, including those in the first century who walked with Jesus, say a rather extraordinary thing about him; they say he is the Son of God.

Other people, even some folks who want to call themselves Christians, say that we are all sons of God and that Jesus was just one of us, though perhaps a bit more spiritual. If that were the claim made about him, we would not bother looking at him twice, but it is quite clear that the New Testament teaches that Jesus had a unique type of sonship. The Bible says that he preexisted with God the Father before Creation and that he and the Father are One. No one else has ever made that claim and been taken seriously.

The second claim that we must put on trial is that he rose from the dead and is still alive, living in heaven. In the past forty years or so we have been hearing of people who were pronounced clinically dead and then brought back to life. Again, if that were the claim made about Jesus, we would not bother to take a second look. Those out-of-body experiences cannot be called resurrections; they are resuscitations, which usually occur within three minutes after the vital signs have stopped or the person is gone. Also, if they "come back," they are still the same person in every detail as before, and they eventually die.

In the case of Jesus, however, it is said that he was dead three days, not three minutes, and that he came back as a different kind of person, yet the same person. Witnesses also saw him ascend from the earth.

Bring On The Witnesses

The primary evidences for these claims are ancient documents written in the generation after the death of

Jesus. Most of the material was recorded by two of the twelve apostles, Matthew and John, and by two other early Christians, Mark and Luke. Other books of the New Testament – the letters of Paul, John, Peter, and James – also present important evidence.

Right from the outset we have a potential problem that any astute attorney would spot. Are these witnesses prejudiced so that we cannot use their testimony? That is, have they already prejudged the case so we cannot be sure of their objectivity? After all, they were all followers of Jesus. Should they be thrown out of the court because they knew him so well? Before we do that, let us think a little more deeply.

One of the writers, Luke, was a Gentile, not a part of the Jewish community from which the first Christians came. He was also a keen-minded doctor and even today considered to be one of the greatest historians ever to live. How did he become a Christian? He searched out the facts of the life of Jesus before he made his decision. Does it not stand to reason that anyone who became convinced that Jesus was the Son of God risen from the dead would eagerly become a Christian? Is not that person, in fact, a better witness than the one who has not made the effort to study these claims?

In courts of law today we always rely on witnesses; we do not dismiss them as being biased because they saw the person or event. Imagine a lawyer saying, "Your honor, I object to the evidence of this witness because he believes what he is saying!"

John also was certain Jesus was no ordinary human being. Why?

For one thing, he had been to the Mount of Transfiguration (Mark 9:1-8), where he had seen Jesus glorified and had heard the voice from heaven commending Jesus as *my beloved Son* (KJV).

John and Luke did not bear witness just because they were Christians; rather, they were Christians because they had been convinced through experience and examination. It misses the point entirely to say they are not valid sources for evidence because they were prejudiced. Their lives had been totally changed by their discovery of this truth about Jesus, and that is why they wrote. If they had not been radically affected, they would not have bothered to do all that writing. The same can be said of the other New Testament authors.

Now The Evidence

Consider the evidence that supports the claim that Jesus was uniquely the Son of God. The gospel writers all agree that Jesus himself said he was the Son of God:

> ➢ *The Jews picked up stones again to stone Him. Jesus answered them, "I showed you many good works from the Father; for which of them are you stoning Me?" The Jews answered Him, "For a good work we do not stone You, but for blasphemy; and because You, being a man, make Yourself out to be God." Jesus answered them, "Has it not been written in your Law, 'I said, you are gods'? If he called them gods, to whom the word of God came (and the Scripture cannot be broken), do you say of Him, whom the Father sanctified and sent into the world, 'You are blaspheming,' because I said, 'I*

am the Son of God'? If I do not do the works of My Father, do not believe Me; but if I do them, though you do not believe Me, believe the works, so that you may know and understand that the Father is in Me, and I in the Father" (John 10:31-38).

➤ *The woman said, "I know that Messiah is coming. (He who is called Christ); when that One comes, He will declare all things to us." Jesus said to her, "I who speak to you am He"* (John 4:25,26).

➤ *But He kept silent and did not answer. Again the high priest was questioning Him, and saying to Him, "Are You the Christ, the Son of the Blessed One?" And Jesus said, "I am; and you shall see the Son of Man sitting at the right hand of Power, and coming with the clouds of heaven." Tearing his clothes, the high priest said, "What further need do we have of witnesses? You have heard the blasphemy; how does it seem to you?" And they all condemned Him to be deserving of death* (Mark 14:61-64).

➤ *When it was day, the Council of elders of the people assembled, both chief priests and scribes, and they led Him away to their council chamber, saying, "If You are the Christ, tell us." But He said to them, "If I tell you, you will not believe; and if I ask a question, you will not answer. But from now on the Son of Man will be seated at the right hand of the power of God." And they all said, "Are You the Son of God, then?" And He said to them, "Yes, I am." Then they said, "What further need do we have of testimony? For we have heard it ourselves from His own mouth."* (Luke 22:66-71).

Jesus claimed to be not only the Messiah, but also the Son of God. Ultimately it was the latter claim that incited the Jews to want him dead.

Beside what Jesus said about himself, there are other types of evidence regarding the claim that he was the Son of God, notably his many acts of power over nature, seen in the calming of the winds of the sea, multiplying loaves of bread and fish from a small picnic basket to feed more than five thousand hungry people, walking on water, and filling fishermen's nets so full they were ready to break open. Numerous supernatural healings occurred at his command. Lepers were cleansed; blind men were made to see; cripples were given strong, healthy legs; and surely most spectacular of all, Lazarus was raised after having been dead for four days. These pieces of evidence must be considered carefully as we look at the claim that Jesus was the Son of God.

Many of the events surrounding the birth, life, and death of Jesus were predicted hundreds of years earlier, conforming to the expectation of the Messiah:

➢ his birth in Bethlehem (Micah 5:2)
➢ his coming from the tribe of Judah (Genesis 49:10)
➢ his suffering and death (Isaiah 53:1-12)
➢ his working miracles (Isaiah 35:5,6)
➢ his birth by a virgin (Isaiah 7:14)
➢ his flight to Egypt (Hosea 11:1)
➢ his triumphal entry into Jerusalem (Zechariah 9:9,10)

> ➤ his being sold for thirty pieces of silver (Zechariah 11:12)
> ➤ and many of the details of his death (Isaiah 53:7; 50:6; 53:12; Psalm 22:1-8, 16, 18)

All these events were fulfilled by Jesus of Nazareth, demonstrating that he was the One predicted by the prophets to be the Messiah, or God's Son.

What Character!

The character of Jesus also offers a clue to his identity. If we can find character flaws or sinful actions in his life, we could dismiss the claim that Jesus is the Son of God. But what do we find when we look at his life? It is true that he was tempted, but he did not yield to those temptations (Matthew 4:1-11). We have no record of his sinning. He claimed point-blank to his enemies that he was sinless. *Which one of you convicts Me of sin?* (John 8:46), he asked the Pharisees. But there was no reply or suggestion that he had done any specific sin.

Instead he had an opposite effect on people. The sinful became righteous; the ignorant became eloquent orators; the greedy became generous; skeptics became convinced believers; social outcasts became respectable citizens! The effect he had on people seems to have been most wholesome.

Sabbath Changers

Another area of evidence would be any lasting effects Jesus had on the community of people who were his followers. After his death, the number of his disciples kept growing, and groups called churches came into being all over the Roman Empire. Now these people did not gather just to perpetuate the memory of a dead hero. They were, in fact, worshipping him. So phenomenal was the spread of the movement that within a few hundred years, Christianity became the official religion of the Roman Empire.

Another remarkable change had to do with the day of worship. The Jews had very strict laws about observing the Sabbath, which is the last day of the week, Saturday. But very early, many Christian Jews were found observing Sunday, the first day of the week, as the Lord's Day. For a Jew to tamper with the Sabbath was almost like committing spiritual suicide. Something quite significant must have caused them to change. That "something" was the fact that Sunday was the day they claimed Jesus rose from the dead. Throughout the world Christians began meeting on Sundays for worship, as they still do.

One other strand of historical evidence is the Christian book, or New Testament. Its existence is a testimony to the fact that first-century people really believed Jesus was who he said he was, the Son of God. In summary then, we have the first-person claims of Jesus, miracles of many varieties, fulfilled Old Testament prophecy, the impeccable character of Jesus, the followers of Jesus who were radically changed, the growth of the Church, Sunday worship, and the New Testament—all as evidence that Jesus is the Son of God.

To The Jurors' Room

Members of the jury, given all that evidence, what other possibilities are there regarding the identity of Jesus? If he was not the Son of God, who or what was he?

Well, some people considered him to have been a great prophet. Others said he was an agent of the devil. Some thought it possible that he was an imposter or liar, perhaps an egomaniac out to win a place for himself in the history books, or perhaps rather than trying to fool others, he himself was fooled or self-deceived, a lunatic. Others have said that he was just a legendary figure, greatly exaggerated by his disciples who were trying to "con" the rest of the world. Maybe Matthew, Mark, Luke, John, Peter, James, and Paul got together to form a new club for those who were tired of all the laws and sacrifices of Judaism. So they made up all the stories of Jesus' healing the sick, raising the dead, walking on water. Maybe Jesus was the subject of a "tall tale" like Paul Bunyan or Robin Hood. So we have these possibilities: great prophet, agent of Satan, liar, lunatic, and legendary figure.[13]

A Prophet?

Jesus came with a prophetic message and, in his earliest days, was associated with a prophet, John the Baptist. Remember, however, that even John the Baptist said Jesus was the Messiah, the Lamb of God, and the Son of God (John 1:26,29,34). Could John have been wrong? Could Peter also have been wrong, when in Matthew 16:16 after others suggested that Jesus was just a prophet, Peter cried out, *Thou art the Christ, the Son of the living God*?

Some non-Christian religions today that want to pay great respect to Jesus but to not accept the evidence of history or the other evidences we cited above consider him to have been just a prophet. Some may still be looking for a messiah. Those closest to Jesus in history and in relationship did not accept this point of view; in fact, many of them died horrific martyr deaths because they insisted that Jesus rose from the dead.

A Satanic Agent?

Some of those who observed the miracles of Jesus accused him of having a demon (John 8:48) or of casting out demons by the power of Satan (Matthew 12:24). His answer was a powerful argument against that idea; *If Satan casts out Satan, he is divided against himself* (v. 26). Surely Satan is clever enough not to work against himself. Besides, the teachings of Jesus do not sound as if they came from an evil man.

A Liar?

For this to be a possibility, we would have to have a motive for Jesus' inventing such a lie. Maybe, as we said earlier, he was an egomaniac trying to write himself into history. There certainly were many false messiahs in the days of Jesus. When we look at what Jesus did when some people tried to make him a king, we have to eliminate that motive. He totally rejected them (John 6:15). He told Pilate at his trial that it was not his intention to create an earthly kingdom (John 18:36).

Perhaps he had another motive of which we are not aware. Is there any evidence that would suggest that he purposely was deceiving his followers? Some of his miracles defied any explanation. Jesus could not come to his disciples and say, "Hey, guys, guess what I did yesterday! I raised our friend Lazarus from the dead," unless, of course, he had really done it. There is no way he could tell a lie about that kind of thing, for it would have been easy to contradict him and expose him.

The idea that Jesus may have been a liar fails to note that Jesus was the founder and teacher of the greatest ethical system the world has ever known. The teachings of Jesus on human behavior contain the most noble thoughts and wisest words ever given to help the human family live in the best possible way. Does it make sense that the author of such lofty teaching was himself a liar? One of the basic truths of Christian teaching on behavior is honesty or truthfulness. Jesus both spoke the truth and was the Truth (John 14:6).

A Lunatic?

Could it be that rather than trying to deceive others, Jesus himself was deceived regarding his identity? Perhaps he honestly thought he was the Son of God, but was sadly mistaken. There are always people who do not know who they really are. Some are put away in institutions because they are so out of touch with reality. Does Jesus strike us as being like that? A psycho case? Often he healed those with mental problems. Again, consider his high level of teaching and fantastic miracles. A self-deceived man cannot talk himself into doing miracles.

One writer has commented that at the most crucial moment of his life, under intense pressure with his very life at stake, Jesus appeared calm, cool, collected, and in control. An unhealthy mind would totally collapse in such a moment. His mind, with which even the greatest Jewish intellectuals could not contend, made those who put him on trial feel as though they were the ones being tried. No, Christians for the last two thousand years have not put their belief in a lunatic. Or a liar. Or a devil. Or even a prophet.

But there is one more possibility that could undermine his claims, which we examine in the next chapter.

Chapter 11

The Final Verdict

We have had the claims of Jesus on trial. Is he truly the one that Christians have claimed him to be for nearly twenty centuries? Is he the Messiah and Son of God? Is he alive? We have examined and dismissed several hypotheses already, but we now come to the last possibility, which may be the most difficult of all.

Some people believe that Jesus never claimed to be the Son of God. This theory argues that his followers who wrote the New Testament purposely made a legend out of him to perpetuate his memory, for they saw many great qualities in him. They saw his great power and heard his great teachings and then decided that, surely, he could not have been just a normal man. When they wrote the New Testament books, they exaggerated the stories to make Jesus into more of a hero than he actually was. Then they went on to try to convince the public that he was the Messiah and the Son of God.

In other words, this theory suggests that the disciples of Jesus pulled off the greatest "con" job in history, and that hundreds of millions of people over hundreds of years have been thoroughly duped.

The reason this theory is harder to handle than the others is that it discredits the witnesses and leaves us with no written evidence about Jesus that we can trust. If the Gospel writers were conspiring to make us think Jesus was the Son of God, we cannot accept their word that Jesus performed miracles and rose from the dead. Is it possible that the real founders of Christianity are the gospel writers, not Jesus, and that the Gospels are "tall tales" rather than true reports? Many people believe so, but they fail to consider two facts that a good lawyer would quickly present.

First, it is quite impossible to "pull off" a hoax when thousands of people are watching. There were too many intelligent people aware of the life and teachings of Jesus who desperately wanted the Jesus movement to end in the tomb with Jesus. Surely, it is impossible to create a legend in one generation, as author Paul Little points out.[14] It takes many generations for a legend to develop.

"I Like Ike"

In the early 1950's the President of the United States was Dwight Eisenhower (Ike), a very popular man. He had been a hero in the war, and then as a politician, he won the presidency twice.

Now suppose someone would come around today (a real Ike fan) and say, "Citizens of the world, here is some great news which you ought to believe. About seventy years ago there was a man named Dwight Eisenhower who was the Son of God. You did not realize it at the time, but he really was the Son of God. Here are some things about him: he was born of a virgin; lived a sinless life; did fantastic miracles like walking on water, calming storms, changing water into wine, and feeding thousands with just a few hamburgers. He also healed cripples, lepers, schizophrenics, deaf, blind, and he even raised the dead. After he died, he rose from the dead. Dwight Eisenhower – I want you to believe in him, commit your life to him, and be willing to die for him. In fact, we are going to start a new religion—the Eisenhower Evangelical Church. Become a believer, and then you will have real Eisenhower-power!"

Now that is ridiculous. Why?

There are thousands of people still alive today who knew Eisenhower. Our parents and grandparents may have liked Ike and even voted for him, but they would tell us quite quickly that Mr. Eisenhower was not the Son of God, not the Messiah, and not even a saint. If someone were to try to build a legend about him like that in one generation, anyone who wanted to examine such claims could go to people who knew the man to find out the truth.

In the case of Jesus, if someone wanted to doubt Matthew's word, all he had to do was go back to Galilee or Jerusalem and say, "Hey, anybody around here ever know a guy named Jesus of Nazareth? What kind of chap was he? Did he really do miracles?" If people who were eyewitnesses to his life said, "No, he wasn't like that; he didn't do those things; he was just an ordinary Jew," that would have been the end of it. The Jesus movement would have stopped right there. No believers, no church; curtains on Christianity. But, obviously, that was not the case. Jesus was not just a legendary hero. It is impossible to create a legend in one generation.

The Verdict

We have considered many options regarding the identity of Jesus. We have seen on the positive side:

1. He claimed to be the Son of God.
2. He did many miracles.
3. He fulfilled Old Testament prophecy about the Messiah.
4. He lived a sinless life.
5. His followers became new people.
6. Many of them died grisly martyr deaths.
7. His disciples have been multiplying into a worldwide church.
8. His resurrection changed the day of worship.
9. His followers left written records that are irrefutable.

On the negative side, we have seen that it is impossible to believe that he was:

1. Just an ordinary man
2. A great prophet
3. An agent of the devil
4. A lying egomaniac

5. A self-deceived lunatic
6. A legendary hero

So, who was he? We have been quite thorough in this trial, and from the legal point of view, from all the evidence, we must come to the conclusion that Jesus was who he said he was – the Son of God. To believe anything else is to be dishonest, gullible, or thoughtless. Case dismissed! In fact, this is exactly the conclusion reached by a brilliant British journalist some years ago. Frank Morison was sympathetic to the person of Jesus, but he was quite convinced that Jesus was no more that a truly good man. Morison hoped that by carefully examining the events of Jesus' life the week before the crucifixion, it would be possible to better understand why such a preposterous story had been believed by so many.

The title of the first chapter of Morison's book, *Who Moved the Stone?*[15], gives a clue to his findings: "The Book That Refused to be Written." From his investigative efforts, Morison concluded that the Christians had it right all along. The evidence we will now consider in the second case was so compelling that Morison moved from being a skeptic to being a thoroughly convinced Christian.

Next Case

The second claim about Jesus for us to investigate has to do with his destiny. If all that we have said about his identity is true but it all ended in a Judean tomb, we twenty-first century people would look back and admire, but find no meaning for us. In fact, if the body of Jesus still occupies a tomb, the rest of what we have said about him is put in jeopardy because one of his claims was that he would rise from the dead as a Victor, not a victim.

We convene our court again to examine this most extraordinary claim – that a man who died a cruel, bloody death by execution walked out of a sealed-up tomb in perfect health three days later. If that happened, the whole meaning of history and human life changes!

When we try to find witnesses to this astonishing miracle of the resurrected Jesus, we are surprised at how many we have! The women, who went to the tomb very early on the Sunday morning that we now call the first Easter, were Mary Magdalene, Mary the mother of James, and Salome (Mark 16:1). Their purpose was to anoint the corpse; this fact is very important, as we will see later.

Next were Peter and John, who ran to the tomb after hearing Mary's report (John 20:2-4); they found it empty also. But so far all we have is an empty tomb, which does not prove anything. Strangely enough, Peter and John did see the graveclothes, and some Bible scholars believe that John's report (John 20:5-7) suggests that the linens had not been unwrapped, but were empty. That would be extremely significant.

Mary Magdalene, among the first to discover the empty tomb, was also given the honor of being the first to see the risen Jesus. Thus far, we have one witness. Next, we learn about Jesus coming alongside two weary and puzzled disciples, Cleopas and another (Luke 24:13-35). They had heard the report of the empty tomb, but they were skeptical until Jesus revealed himself to them – three witnesses now. Later in the evening he went among all the apostles except Thomas (and Judas, who was now dead) – thirteen eyewitnesses now. Doubting Thomas got a special audience with the risen Lord eight days later, making a total of fourteen thus far.

These were not one-time visits Jesus paid these people. Luke, John, and Matthew suggest that there were several other appearances to these early disciples. Nor were they just appearances, as in a dream or vision. Jesus spoke with them, was touched by them, ate with them (Luke 24:36-43), and gave some very personal teaching to them (John 21; Matthew 28). This occurred over a period of forty days (Acts 1:3). In all, the Gospels report that Jesus appeared twelve times prior to his ascension.

We also learn from Paul that Jesus appeared to *more than five hundred brethren at one time* (1 Corinthians 15:6), which does not allow us to have a precise figure, but certainly adds to the evidence substantially. For the sake of our tally, let us assume five hundred plus our previous fourteen. One more must be added – the Apostle Paul, himself, who said, *he appeared to me also* (1 Corinthians 15:8; see also Acts 9:1-9). So, there we have it—at least 515 eyewitnesses of the living Jesus Christ after his crucifixion.

The Alternatives

Now let's consider the other side of this case, which assumes that dead men, including Jesus, do not rise. How shall we account for the evidence we have just seen? We will list the possibilities and take them one at a time:

1. He was never dead.
2. His body was stolen.
3. The women went to the wrong tomb.

The first idea is that Jesus did not die on the cross but rather went into a deep coma. This has been called the swoon theory, which suggests that in the "beautiful calm of the cool tomb" Jesus regained consciousness and adequately revived so that he could make his exit from the tomb. It does not take much deep thinking to see how preposterous this idea is. Seven facts must be considered.

First, we remember that besides hanging on the cross for six hours, Jesus had his side pierced by a Roman spear so that blood and water gushed out. Medical authorities tell us that this separation of blood and water is itself proof that Jesus was already dead. The spear in the side would have been enough to kill him even without crucifixion.

Second, those Roman soldiers were not "green-horns" in the grisly art of crucifixion; they knew a dead man when they saw one. They were not about to take a man down from the cross unless he were dead. In fact, because Joseph of Arimathea wanted to bury the body before the sundown of Sabbath, he needed permission from Pilate to take the body from the cross. Before giving Joseph such permission, Pilate called the centurion to ascertain from him that Jesus was, in fact, dead (Mark 15:42-45).

Third, Joseph and Nicodemus wrapped Jesus in linens with myrrh and aloes weighing about seventy-five pounds. Then they wrapped a tight turban around his head and face—hardly ideal circumstances for reviving!

Fourth, while the tomb may have been calm and peaceful, it would have been cold and damp on an April evening in Palestine. Between the graveclothes and this unfavorable climate, even if Jesus had not been dead when put into the tomb, he would have died, not revived.

Assuming, contrary to all we have just said, that Jesus did not die but did indeed revive in the tomb, we have the fifth problem of the stone in front of the tomb. How was it moved? It is inconceivable to think that in such a wounded, battered condition, Jesus could have budged that stone.

Even if he did, as a sixth point, can we imagine him overcoming the guards who were there on Pilate's orders to see that no one tampered with the tomb? Had he somehow emerged from the tomb in his beaten, battered, weakened state, they would have quickly executed him on the spot and put him back in the tomb, for their own necks were on the line with the rulers.

Seventh, had he overcome the spear wound, the graveclothes, the cold tomb, the huge rock, and the guards, can you now see him limping badly on those nail-pierced feet along the dusty roads for miles to present himself believably to the disciples as the glorious, all-conquering, resurrected Lord? The disciples were not stupid or gullible. He would desperately have needed medical attention and much care. Far from appearing as victor, he would have seemed a pathetic victim. All these factors indicate that Jesus was dead beyond all doubt. He did die on the cross. It takes more faith to believe he did not die than to believe he rose from death!

Grave Raiders

The second theory is that the dead body of Jesus was stolen. But who would have stolen it and why? Matthew tells us that the Jews were worried that the disciples would snatch the body and then say Jesus rose from death, so

Pilate allowed them to make the grave as secure as they wanted.

Now on the next day, the day after the preparation, the chief priests and the Pharisees gathered together with Pilate, and said, "Sir, we remember that when He was still alive that deceiver said, 'After three days I am to rise again.' Therefore, give orders for the grave to be made secure until the third day, otherwise His disciples may come and steal Him away and say to the people, 'He has risen from the dead,' and the last deception will be worse than the first." Pilate said to them, "You have a guard; go, make it as secure as you know how." And they went and made the grave secure, and along with the guard they set a seal on the stone (Matthew 27:62-66).

For the moment, let us assume that the guards failed in their mission. Perhaps they all fell asleep, or were distracted somehow. Then sometime in the night the disciples came, rolled back the stone, unwrapped the linens from the body, wrapped them all up again (Why?), and then made off with the body. They then, theoretically, reburied the body somewhere else, found a Jesus look-alike somewhere, and bribed him to play the role of the living Lord so as to deceive all the others. The story would have spread like wildfire that Jesus was alive, and these deceptive disciples would have gone to their own graves years later knowing that they had pulled off a great hoax.

Wait a minute. How did these lying followers go to their graves? History tells us that apart from John, they all died violent martyr deaths because of their belief in the resurrection of Jesus. Now men will die willingly for noble causes of which they are convinced, but no man lays down his life for what he knows to be a lie. Surely just at the point of greatest threat they would have "cracked" and admitted that it was all a hoax, that they knew Jesus was not alive. But that did not happen. They went to their martyr deaths willingly, knowing they were joining the resurrected, ascended, and glorified Jesus! The disciples did not steal the corpse.

The only possible other grave-raiders would have been the Jews or the Romans. Obviously, the Jews did not do it. As we have seen, it was their desire to keep the grave closed so that the Jesus movement would end in the tomb with the dead body of Jesus. If, however, they had some other reason to snatch away the body, the Jews would have merely shown the corpse when the disciples started claiming, *He is risen*. So, it was not the Jews.

What about the Romans? First, we would have to think of a motive for their stealing the body. They were no friends of Christianity either. Again, once the resurrection claims were being made, all they needed to do was have a public viewing of the corpse.

On the contrary, belief in the resurrected Lord spread so rapidly that in a few hundred years, Christianity was proclaimed the official religion of the whole Roman Empire. Obviously, no one stole the body of Jesus.

Hysterical Women

The only other theory is that the women who first proclaimed the resurrection gave a false report. This idea suggests that the Marys and Salome went to the wrong tomb in the darkness of the early dawn. There they saw an empty tomb and, because they desired so much for

Jesus to be alive, when a gardener spoke to Mary later, she assumed he was Jesus. Her hysterical report was brought to the disciples, who also came to the same wrong tomb. That is how the fantasy got started, according to the theory.

Several facts, however, discredit this view. First, as we saw earlier, far from expecting to see Jesus alive, Mary came carrying embalming spices. While we may conceive of one hysterical person talking herself into believing a loved one had been resurrected, we cannot allow that 514 others were also so duped and self-deceived. Also, we have the certainty that the Jews and Romans would have paraded out the body for all to see once the word started spreading that Jesus was alive. Surely, they knew where the tomb was. But as a matter of fact, the right tomb was an empty tomb!

Case Dismissed

We therefore rule, having explored the evidence, and affirm with billions of Christians over the past twenty centuries in nearly every nation on earth that, as the Apostles' Creed says, *Jesus Christ WAS CRUCIFIED, DEAD, AND BURIED ... THE THIRD DAY HE ROSE AGAIN FROM THE DEAD.*

Chapter 12

Conversion God's Way

Finding good news in the newspaper or internet these days is a very rare event. Terrorism, political assassinations, famines, earthquakes, highway accidents, racial upheavals, global economic woes all appear regularly in the news. It confirms our belief that there is not much good news to report in the affairs of mankind. But we have been considering eternal good news, called the gospel.

How does the gospel come to us today? The primary way of communicating the good news is the preaching of the gospel. Now, that does not necessarily mean standing behind the pulpit Sunday morning and delivering a half-hour sermon, although that is a great place for it to be done. The word *preach* literally means proclaim. It means to bring an announcement. If you combine the two words *preach* and *gospel,* you have the announcement of good news.

Proclamation of good news – that is what preaching is supposed to be about. Anyone who knows the good news can be a "preacher." The good news should be shared at work (on your own time), in school, on the athletic field, in homes – everywhere you go where people do not know Jesus personally. Every Christian can be a proclaimer of the good news.

What's In It For Me?

What does the gospel provide for those who accept it? For one thing, the gospel brings enlightenment. People in our day want to understand what life is all about. Without knowing God on a personal, experiential level, it is impossible to understand fully what life is about or why God created us in the world.

Often people wonder, "Why would God bother to create a world and create people?" I have answered that question by asking why did I want children? I want to enjoy them, and I do. I love to love them. And that's the way God is. God desires to have people to enjoy. People who do not know God personally cannot really fellowship with him or enjoy his presence with them, and so they are not fulfilling their purpose.

Another provision of the gospel is the hope of eternal life. God gives us life instead of eternal death. In fact, he created us to be immortal, but sin made us mortal; we get sick and we die. The gospel nullifies the eternal impact of both sin and death.

If you have responded to the gospel, you should be noticing God's power at work in you in many aspects of your life. When you are in contact with people who do not know God nor want to please him, you will see that they do not have the ability to live as they know they should because they lack the power of God. The gospel gives power for self-control.

The gospel provides peace, real peace, so that we do not have to worry and fret about our lives or destinies. Many people worry about where they are going when they die. The gospel gives us firm assurance that we are safe because we are saved.

Conversion: First Consideration

In chapters 5 and 9 we considered salvation, what it is and what is means, but how does one gain it? Let us consider this by reviewing a story found in Acts 16.

When Paul and Silas first set foot on European soil, they came to Philippi, where they were thrown into jail for preaching the gospel. In jail they were singing and praising God when the Lord delivered them miraculously through an earthquake. They could have escaped, but decided to stay. Had they left, the jailor would have been executed because his prisoners had escaped. When the jailor found that Paul and the other prisoners were still there, he asked the most profound question that can be asked: *What must I do to be saved?* Apparently, he had already heard the message to some extent because he knew salvation was a real issue in his life. *What must I do to be saved?* was his deep concern.

In order to be saved, there are certain steps we must take to benefit from God's provision. We must cooperate with God. Our salvation is not the result of our works, but of God's provision and our response to him.

About Face!

The first part of conversion is repentance. In mathematics, if you had a fraction like 13/16, and the teacher said, "Convert this to a decimal," what did she mean? Your teacher really was telling you to change the fraction into another form. Instead of having a numerator and denominator, you calculated a decimal figure (.8125 in this case; I used my calculator). Conversion means changing from one form to another.

In the biblical sense, conversion deals specifically with our mind. When you come to God wanting to be made right with him, it is not enough to say, "God, I am bad. Please forgive me and help me to be good." We need to go beyond that and truly repent.

The Greek word for *repent* has two parts. The first part is *change;* the second part is *mind.* Repent means to change your mind about your sin. Whereas in the past you enjoyed your sin and thought it was all right, now you despise the sin and you are very sorry that you have been sinful. The first part of conversion, repentance, is a complete change of mind, doing an about face in your life, a 180 degree turn, a full *you* -turn.

The best illustration of the word *conversion* is the caterpillar. Early in life this ugly, fuzzy thing creeps along, being very vulnerable. You can step on him, and that's it. He cannot fly away; he cannot fight back; all he can do is go squish.

The caterpillar, however, (if it does not go squish) one day spins a cocoon and eventually flies away with wings of a butterfly. That is just like conversion.

In a sense, all of us are like creeping caterpillars before we are saved. We do not have any wings to get off the ground spiritually. When we become a Christian, when Christ comes into our life, and our spirit is reborn, we receive wings – spiritual wings – to get off the ground into the life of the Spirit.

Bad Boys Included

Luke 15 contains a great story of repentance. A young man had an older brother and a father who was quite wealthy. The disrespectful younger brother got a little bored living on the family farm and said, "Hey, Dad, even though I'm not scheduled to receive my inheritance until you die, give it to me now. I want to go do my own thing" (rough paraphrase of Luke 15:12ff). Although the father was grieved about this, he agreed to do it. The son took his inheritance, left home, and spent it in wild living.

Fortunately, when he saw what was happening to him, he repented. He acknowledged that he was messed up. That is the first part of repentance, being honest about your situation. He then recognized that he had deeply hurt his father and felt great sorrow in his own heart because of it. Repentance without sorrow is incomplete. Repentance is not just asking to be forgiven. That can be done on a very rational, intellectual level. Repentance includes the emotions because it involves sorrow. Realizing he had hurt his father, and feeling sorry about that, he got up and went home. He said, *I will get up and go to my father, and will say to him, "Father, I have sinned against heaven, and in your sight;"* (Luke 15:18). He left his sinful environment and his sinful ways and returned to the father. All of that is involved in full repentance.

Repent Or Perish

One of the tragedies of overeager evangelism today is the high-pressure salesmanship that says, "All you need to do to get saved is to pray, 'Dear Lord, I know I'm a sinner; I know Jesus died to forgive me of my sins. Please come into my heart and cleanse me and save me.'" In this, there is no heart, no emotion, no sorrow for sin. It can be just a mechanical formula. That is sad because no one can really enjoy salvation unless he understands the depths from which he has been saved. Maybe that's why so many conversions seem to be stillbirths.

Is it really necessary to repent in order to be saved? The answer is yes.

When Peter preached at Pentecost, 3,000 people were convicted of their sin. They said, *What shall we do?* He said, *Repent and let each of you be baptized in the name of Jesus Christ for the forgiveness of your sins, and you shall receive the gift of the Holy Spirit* (Acts 2:38). It is necessary to repent – to change our minds about sin, and then decide not to sin.

Repentance is not salvation itself; it is just the beginning of salvation. Jesus one time said, *Unless you repent, you too will all likewise perish* (Luke 13:3). It is not an arbitrary thing for some people to repent and others not. The truth of the matter is that nobody is saved unless he repents.

Have you ever seen a person who prays for forgiveness and asks God to save him from his sin, but experiences no change in his life? I have seen many people like that. They make the prayer, go through the motions, but do not seem to change at all. It is as though nothing had happened. The reason may be that they did not repent. Perhaps they asked for salvation, but had no deep sorrow for their sin; they did not mix their faith with repentance.

Faith: Beyond Repentance

What is necessary besides repentance? Beyond repentance is faith. Notice this formula: repentance + faith = conversion.

In the Bible the words *faith* and *believe* are the same word in Greek. Faith means to accept the truth in such a way that you believe it to be actually true. More than that, you act upon it, convinced that it is true. For example, the weatherman may say, "It is going to snow tomorrow starting at noon. We are going to have an accumulation of five to eight inches of snow." If you believe him, have faith in him, you will dress accordingly – wear boots and winter togs. If you wear sneakers or sandals, by that act you are saying, "I do not believe him." If he was right, and you did not believe him, you would come home trudging in your sneakers through six inches of snow. To have faith means to act according to what you believe.

No person who says she has faith in Jesus is speaking the truth unless she has trusted Jesus to forgive her of her sin. No person can say he believes in Jesus unless he has been converted, and no person has been converted unless he has trusted Jesus to save him.

Belief is not just believing facts; it is not just accepting certain truths. An atheist can believe a man named Jesus was born in Bethlehem about 2000 years ago. He can believe that he did many wonderful things and died on a cross. An atheist can believe that. The Bible says that the devil himself believes in God and trembles, but neither the devil nor an atheist is saved because neither has put faith into his belief.

Exercising Saving Faith

John 1:12 says: *but as many as received Him, to them He gave the right to become children of God, even to those who believe in His name.* The three verbs in that verse are important. To those who have *received* him, who have *believed* in his name, he gave the right to *become* children of God. There is someone to be received, something to believe, and something to become. All of these have their part in saving faith.

How do I exercise this kind of faith? Suppose one day as you are driving along you see a group of teens playing hockey on a frozen pond. They are examples of faith in action as they glide around playing hockey on the pond. Their faith is in the strength of the ice. We might wonder if they have a lot of faith or little faith, but what does it matter? What really matters is the thickness of the ice.

Many people talk about needing more faith, but that is irrelevant to salvation. The issue is not how much faith we have but how adequate our God is. If we have a little God, we would be foolish to put a lot of faith in him. Or to go back to the pond idea, it would be foolish to put a lot of faith in ice only half an inch thick. The skaters would turn out to be very wet, very cold and maybe very drowned. If the ice was three feet thick, they might go out in fear and trembling with only a little bit of faith, but it would not matter, for the ice would still hold up. It is not the amount of faith we have that is important; it is the adequacy of the object of our faith. But some faith is essential.

Saving faith is trusting in what we know to be true about God. The Bible says, *if you confess Jesus as Lord, and believe in your heart that God raised Him from the dead; you shall be saved* (Romans 10:9). If you confess with your mouth and believe with your heart, you are saved. When you repent and have faith, the result is that your whole life begins to change.

Consider the diagram at the end of this chapter called *Crucial Steps in Christian Conversion.* Notice at the top there is a triangle that represents God. In step one, you are unconscious of the fact that God wants to relate to you. You know that you are alive and that God exists, but you are not alive to God.

Step two is the discovery of Christ. You become aware that Jesus Christ exists. You are separated from him, but you understand that he exists and believe intellectually that he is God's provision for salvation.

Step three is where conversion takes place. You see that Christ has come down to earth on your level and that if you receive him, you will enter into a relationship with him that begins a great change. Notice the arrow in both directions – the arrow coming down from Christ and the arrow going up from you. This refers to your trusting in and receiving Christ and to God's forgiving you and giving you the right to become his child. You give yourself to him and receive full salvation.

This involves action on Christ's part, which he has already completed by dying at Calvary to make forgiveness possible. On the cross, Jesus Christ suffered the judgment of God on your sin. It also involves action on your part in giving yourself to him and receiving forgiveness. It involves repenting and trusting Christ. That is the beginning of conversion.

Step four shows you becoming more Christ-like. You are in Christ – that is your unchanging position as a child of God, but you are still in the world. Now, however, Christ is being formed in you, and so there is less and less of you and more and more of Christ. That is Christian growth. The character of Jesus is being formed in you. For example, Jesus wants you to be pure. In your own self, you are not a pure person, but as the character of Christ takes more control, you become purer. So, that fourth step is a lifelong process of growth.

The fifth step is ultimate glorification where Christ and you are one in character. *We shall be like Him, because we shall see Him just as He is* (1 John 3:2).

It is important that you do not merely understand and accept these ideas without responding to them. The gospel is not good news for you if you do not act on it. Perhaps you have responded to it, initially at least, and have gone through step three. The question that you need to ask yourself continually is, where am I in terms of step four? Am I living for myself or am I allowing Christ to be my Lord?

Crucial Steps in Christian Conversion

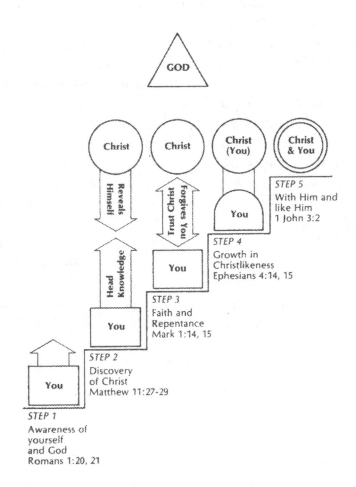

GOD

Christ — Christ — Christ (You) — Christ & You

Reveals Himself

Trust Christ Forgives You

Head Knowledge

You

STEP 5
With Him and
like Him
1 John 3:2

STEP 4
Growth in
Christlikeness
Ephesians 4:14, 15

STEP 3
Faith and
Repentance
Mark 1:14, 15

STEP 2
Discovery
of Christ
Matthew 11:27-29

STEP 1
Awareness of
yourself
and God
Romans 1:20, 21

Chapter 13

Adopted by the Judge

In a church I served was a family that consisted of a father, a mother, seven children born to them, about eight adopted children, and another eight foster children. That is a big family. Twenty-three kids – enough for a full football game, offense and defense, and a kicker. No doubt sometimes life in their household seemed like a football game.

But they were a family. Unless someone told you who was who, you would have no way of knowing which children were born to the parents, which ones were adopted, or which ones were foster children. There were no insiders or outsiders; there were no "pets;" there were no privileged positions. The love that flowed from the parents was like lava from a volcano; it just covered everyone.

That's the way God's love is also. His big family has one natural Son, and millions of adopted sons and daughters.

But it hasn't always been that way. Millions were outsiders with no hope of being included in the family of God. One of the most despairing verses in the Bible is Ephesians 2:12, ... *remember that you were at that time separate from Christ, excluded from the commonwealth of Israel, and strangers to the covenants of promise, having no hope and without God in the world.* Earlier, in the verse 3, these outsiders were described as, *by nature children of wrath.* Paul was saying that outside of Christ Jesus people are orphans in this world. An orphan is a person without parents, perhaps through some tragedy or through being unwanted. In our natural sinful condition, we are not sons and daughters of God but children of wrath. Jesus told the Pharisees that they were of their father the devil, which makes the situation even worse. One of the great truths of Scripture is that as Christians we have been adopted into the family of God.

Often adopted children have a difficult time adjusting to their situations. They have one great benefit, however, that other children do not have. They know that they were personally chosen and wanted by their parents. Those of us born naturally into a family realize that our parents had to take what they got whether they were particularly happy about it or not. An adopted child, on the other hand, is a chosen child.

Jesus told the disciples in John 15:16, *You did not choose Me, but I chose you.* There is a great privilege in being an adopted child, especially if adopted by God. When we are brought into God's family through adoption, we are made joint heirs with Christ Jesus, the Son of God. We are placed as a son or daughter with the full rights and benefits of being royal children. We are welcomed into the family of God with all the privileges, just as if we were naturally born into the household of God.

Before, Now, And Then

When is a person adopted into the family of God? Ephesians 1:5 says that God *predestined us to adoption as sons through Jesus Christ to Himself.* In other words, the decision to adopt us was made long before we were born.

In another sense, however, our adoption takes place at the time we respond to God's grace and are born again of the Spirit into the family of God. Romans 8:15 says that we receive *a spirit of adoption as sons by which we cry out, "Abba! Father!"* Paul stated this just after showing that we become sons of God when we are being led by the Spirit of God. In other words, our adoption occurs at the time of our conversion.

In yet another sense, our adoption is not completed until the time of Christ's Second Coming when our bodies will be redeemed and changed to be like his. In Romans 8:23 Paul encourages us to *wait eagerly for our adoption as sons, the redemption of our body.*

We have this threefold timing of our adoption, but we can rest assured that God accepts us now if we come to him in Christ Jesus. As his sons and daughters, we have full rights and privileges as members of the royal family of the King of kings.

Guilty Until Declared Righteous

Adoption is great, but there are still thousands of children in orphanages. One of my adopted friends used to feel guilty about being adopted, thinking he didn't deserve it when so many others were not chosen. He didn't think it was fair, even though he was grateful.

The question of fairness is an important one in considering the ways of God with humanity. A key biblical term used to discuss it is *justification*. No doubt you have heard *justified* used in normal conversation as referring to fairness. If a friend borrows one of your most prized possessions and then breaks or loses it, you might say that you are justified in expecting him to replace it, meaning that it is only fair or just for your friend to make things right.

Justification in the biblical sense is a technical, legal word. When you are justified, God makes a pronouncement or declaration that you are no longer held guilty for your sin, nor will you be held accountable for it. In fact, the term means even more than that. It includes being made righteous.

In American courts the judge has the right, perhaps with the advice of the jury, to pronounce a person guilty or not guilty. No judge, however, can make a person righteous. Suppose a person is charged with breaking into an Apple store and stealing a computer. He may be brought before the judge and jury and be found innocent of the crime. In reality, he may be guilty; he may have done it, but through dishonest and clever ways was able to show himself innocent. The judge may declare the thief not guilty, but he is not able to make him innocent or righteous. Or, if the accused man did not commit the crime and the jury finds him guilty, that does not mean that he is altogether righteous; it means only that with regard to that one alleged crime he has been found innocent.

In the case of our justification before God, there is absolutely no question about the fact that we are guilty. As John tersely put it, *If we say that we have no sin, we are deceiving ourselves, and the truth is not in us* (1 John 1:8). There is no way we can fool the judge. We stand before the judge with dread, for everyone, ourselves included, knows we are guilty. We are guilty of sin. We have trespassed God's law. We have gone against our own conscience and if we were fair judges, we would condemn ourselves. Because of something very extraordinary, however, the judge is able to say that we are not guilty and, in fact, declare us righteous.

The Judged Judge

The 'something very extraordinary' is the fact that our crime has already been paid for; we have been condemned and sentenced, but as far as God is concerned, the penalty has already paid for our crime.

You say, "How can that be? I've never suffered any great judgment. I have never spent any time in jail." One of the benefits of being a Christian is that we are incorporated into Christ. No longer are we looked upon strictly as individuals. No longer must we stand before the judge in our own names. The judgment, condemnation, and sentence have all been executed upon Jesus Christ. He has paid the full price for us. That is why God can declare you not guilty, for he looks at you as being in Christ; therefore, the penalty has already been paid. Paid in full, on the cross. That's part of the good news of the gospel.

Now here's the strangest irony in the world: since Jesus Christ is God, the judge himself paid the penalty for the convicted sinner. We should always greatly appreciate that fact. It is the only way by which we can be acceptable in God's sight and survive the condemnation we all so rightly deserve. Who has ever heard of a judge convicting a criminal, sentencing him to death, and then pardoning him by saying, "I will take the condemnation that this man rightly deserves?"

It would be incredible to read in the newspaper that a judge went to the gas chamber or a firing squad in the place of a convicted criminal. Yet that really is what happened in the crucifixion of Jesus Christ. He himself bore our sins on the cross.

We know from several Scripture passages that Christians are members or parts of the body of Christ. Because you are part of the body of Christ, you, too, were crucified on Calvary. The whole body of Christ was nailed to the cross; therefore, your penalty has been paid. We need to be careful with this analogy because none of us literally suffered the pain of the cross with Jesus. Nonetheless, God looks upon us as being in Christ in the crucifixion. That is why Paul can say in Galatians 2:20, *I have been crucified with Christ.*

Is It Fair?

But is it fair? Our sense of justice is outraged at the thought of convicted and condemned criminals getting away scot-free. We need, however, to consider to whom or before whom it might be unfair.

Ultimately, God is the judge, and it is his sense of fairness or rightness that counts. What we think is really not that important. If God declares that it is fair to condemn us and sentence us and judge us in Christ Jesus, who are we to say he is wrong? Who are we to say it is not fair? *Shall not the Judge of all the earth deal justly?* (Genesis 18:25). Of course he will. He makes not only the judgment; he also makes the laws and is the standard. If he chooses to justify sinners, that is his sovereign right.

Some people stumble over the idea that a righteous and holy God can justify ungodly and wicked people. Perhaps we all should feel that way so that our appreciation for God's activity in Jesus Christ on our behalf is greater. We must, however, also remember that God's declaration of "not guilty" is not a blanket pardon of all mankind. It applies only to those who are *in Christ Jesus,* who are there on the basis of their repentance and faith in his blood.

Paul, writing to the Romans, made the simple statement that they were justified by faith (Romans 5:1). He also told the Galatians that they were justified not by the works of the law but by faith in Jesus Christ (Galatians 2:16). There is a condition to our being justified, but we must never confuse this with the idea that we have earned or are entitled to justification. It is a gift, a pardon by the Judge himself.

Rather than be scandalized by the thought that a holy and righteous God justifies wicked and ungodly people, we ought to bow our heads and hearts in deep gratitude and live as though we are living on borrowed time, which is exactly the case. Every day is one in which we have been pardoned by God's grace. We must therefore live with the sense that each day is a gift in which we may live for the glory of the One who has forgiven us.

Righteous Frogs

Remember the prince who was a frog until the princess kissed him, which made him a prince once more? In a sense, that story is a good analogy of how being justified has changed us. Earlier we said that justification not only declares us not guilty before God but also makes us righteous in his sight. We are not merely forgiven; we are totally cleansed of all guilt. Prior to being justified, we were all ungodly frogs, but the kiss of God – that is, his grace in our lives – has changed us so that we are princes in his eyes.

This truth will have greater impact upon us when we stand before him on judgment day. We will not stand before him as forgiven criminals, but as righteous sons and daughters. We will be before him just as if we had never sinned. This ought to give us great confidence in our relationship with God now. We need not live continually under the feeling of shame, even though we know that we are forgiven sinners.

Scripture tells us that God not only forgives our sins but also forgets them. In Isaiah 43:25 God says, *I, even I, am the one who wipes out your transgressions for My own sake, and I will not remember your sins.* God does not want us to dwell on past forgiven sins. Since God is omniscient, he knows all things and he reads our minds. By dwelling on past forgiven sins, maybe we keep reminding him of what he says he will forget.

Once we have been forgiven, we should not rehearse the fact of our guilt or dwell upon that sin again in any way. As a result of being justified, we are both declared righteous and made righteous before God. Even though the only person ever to have lived a truly righteous life was our Lord Jesus Christ, incorporation in him means that God sees us the same way he sees Jesus Christ.

Is that fair? No, it's more than fair. It is mercy and grace in action, the love of a Father for his adopted children.

$$Chapter\ 14$$

He Still Heals

One of the important, informal creeds of the day is the "fourfold gospel," four aspects of the gospel or four ways we can experience the Lord Jesus Christ: as Savior, Sanctifier, Healer, and Coming King.[16] We have already considered his provision as Savior. We will consider the other three aspects of the fourfold gospel in this and the next few chapters.

From a theological point of view, all the work of Christ on our behalf is part of salvation, including sanctification, healing and his second coming. Earlier, we saw that in the act of justification God declares us righteous. We are then adopted into his family. Justification and adoption are God's side of providing for our conversion. We become his royal children. Because we are the King's children, we may expect him to take care of us. God has promised to provide and protect us, as any loving father will do. But he can do more than that. He has the ability to heal us. Divine healing is one of the benefits of being in the royal family.

Because of the miraculous and sensational nature of instantaneous physical healing, some unscrupulous religious hucksters have exploited this part of Christian teaching for financial profit or fame. This has made many people skeptical about the teaching of divine healing, including Christians. But healing is clearly one of the ways the Father ministers to his family.

Some Christians assume that divine healing was available only in the days of Jesus and his immediate successors, the apostles. In fact, for centuries the teaching on divine healing lay dormant so that only in the past few generations have Christians again realized that God has provided a way for restoring the health of his children even in contemporary society.

Several famous names may come to mind as we think about people with special healing ministries. Today, healing services are held in churches where a few decades ago such teaching on healing would have been quickly rejected.

In general, God wants his people to be healthy and holy. This is not to suggest that a person who is unhealthy is necessarily out of God's will. God does have purposes for allowing his children to have physical setbacks and even lifelong burdens of pain, suffering and disability, but in a general sense God wants us to enjoy physical health. But how can we know when God wants to heal or why sometimes he does not heal? These are very complex issues – ones that will not allow simplistic answers.

Basic to the question of the possibility of divine healing in our day is the more general question of the possibility of miracles in the twenty first century. While there are some Christians who deny the possibility of miracles in our day, most who believe in a living and active God, the God of the Bible, will admit that God is free to intervene in his creation at any time and in any way he chooses. This allows for miraculous events to occur. If God can miraculously reach into a sinner's life and justify him or her – that is, bring life to a dead spirit – God can just as easily intervene in a person's life in restoring physical health. This is not just a logical assumption; it is also a biblical conclusion.

Scripture affirms that God is not only the creator of the human body but also the sustainer. Ultimately, our lives, physically and spiritually, are God's responsibility. When a believer submits her body to God and gives God total ownership of her body, she is then in the position of being able to look to God to maintain that body which he owns. Miraculous healings still happen. While we cannot say there is a particular method that must be followed before God is free to heal or a particular formula that will force God's hand in the healing, we can, nevertheless, find scriptural teaching that will advise us on the procedure that God expects us to follow when we are seeking him in this way.

Life Out Of Death

The basis for God's healing ministry is the death of our Lord Jesus Christ. When God saves a person, he does not save just a soul. God deals with the whole man or the whole woman. Physical health, therefore, as well as spiritual health, is included in the atonement of Jesus Christ. When God redeems us, he sets free the entire person from sin and its damning effects. Sickness, disease, and suffering, which are ultimately traced back to our being infected by sin, have been dealt with in our Lord's crucifixion. We need, however, to be careful not to assume that any particular person's illness or injury is caused by his or her own personal sins. Jesus made this clear to his disciples in John 9 after they had asked if a particular man was blind because of his own sin or his parents' sin. Jesus said, *It was neither that this man sinned, nor his parents; but it was in order that the works of God might be displayed in him* (John 9:3).

Jesus also reversed this wrong concept when some people told him that Pilate had killed some Galileans. Jesus responded by saying, *Do you suppose that these Galileans were greater sinners than all other Galileans, because they suffered this fare?* (Luke 13:2). Then he reminded them that eighteen people had been killed by the collapse of a tower, and affirmed that they were not worse sinners than others. We need to be very careful not to make hasty judgments when we see particular people suffering with sickness or injury.

On the other hand, we know that suffering and sickness often come from the same source as the sin which separates us spiritually from God. We take comfort in knowing that Christ has dealt with sin through his death on the cross and, therefore, since it is possible to be restored to spiritual health, it is possible to be restored to physical health.

There is one great difference, however, between spiritual healing (salvation) and physical healing. While every person who seeks the Lord for forgiveness and spiritual life is given a positive answer, it is not always true that every believer who seeks the Lord for physical healing is healed. Some well-intentioned but misguided Christians would say that it is only lack of faith that is responsible for a Christian not being healed. Again, we need to be very careful before making such condemning judgments. We know from the case of the Apostle Paul that sometimes God allows us to suffer without choosing to heal us because through that suffering God can do a work in us which he could not otherwise do. He told Paul in 2 Corinthians 12 that he would not heal him because the *"thorn in the flesh"* which God had given him would keep Paul from exalting himself. The Lord added this promise, *My grace is sufficient for you, for power is perfected in weakness (12:9).*

Also, notice in this passage that Paul did specifically ask the Lord for healing. He did not give a wishy-washy, passive prayer, just saying, "Lord, if you want to heal me, I know you can heal me." That is not the kind of asking God desires from us when we come before him. He wants us to ask specifically for healing so that he can give a specific answer. Sometimes, however, that specific answer may be no, as it was in Paul's case. But other times it will be yes.

The faith that God desires in us is bold and honest faith. It does not have to be a big faith, just a rightly placed faith. Ultimately, what matters is not how big our faith in God is, but how big to us is the God of our faith. We can come to God with full confidence that he loves us and will do what is best for us.

Often, this means that he will heal us physically. Our own earthly fathers would not allow us to go on suffering without reason when it would be in their power to correct the situation. Neither will our heavenly Father allow us to suffer without reason. Certainly, restoring us to physical health is within his ability, and often within his will, as I have experienced several times.

The James Prescription

The basic teaching on how one should pursue healing is found in James 5:14-16. James taught that if one is sick, he should *Is anyone among you sick? Then he must call for the elders of the church and they are to pray over him, anointing him with oil in the name of the Lord; and the prayer offered in faith will restore the one who is sick, and the Lord will raise him up, and if he has committed sins, they will be forgiven him. Therefore, confess your sins to one another, and pray for one another so that you may be healed.*

This is neither a magical nor medicinal rite (the oil is not a potion or a medicine); rather, this is a spiritual exercise of discipline and obedience. The discipline comes through confession of sins. The elders themselves are exhorted to confess to one another their sins and to pray for one another, and they are to mix their faith together in praying for and anointing the sick person in the name of the Lord Jesus Christ.

Notice also that it is the responsibility of the sick person to call for the elders of the church. The faith chain begins with the sick person. When God chooses to heal, it is not the elders, their faith, nor the faith of the sick person, nor the oil, nor anything or anyone else that prevails for the sick person. It is the Lord who will raise him up.

In the early days of my ministry I served in a church where there were many different views on healing. Some did not believe healing was available today; others taught that the only reason God would not heal was the lack of faith in the sick person or in the church. Naturally, this caused some tense times, especially when members sought the Lord for healing. When one of our deacons died, suffering a brain aneurysm after a successful kidney transplant, the church went through spiritual trauma. Some were feeling guilty believing they hadn't prayed enough; others wondered why their word of knowledge that Tim would be healed was not true; some condemned the church for raising false expectations, knowing God doesn't heal people today. Most members were hurting and confused.

Clearly, a clear teaching was needed. So, with the elders, we drafted and adopted a paper called *A Personal Inventory for Those Who Seek the Lord for Their Body*.

From then on, we asked people who wanted prayer for healing to answer in writing the questions on the paper. We asked these questions:

➢ What is my PHYSICAL PROBLEM? Please be concrete and specific.

➢ What do I want God to do for me physically? Please be specific.

> ➤ What are my reasons for wanting to be healed? Please list them in order of importance in your own thinking.

> ➤ Please meditate prayerfully on the following Scriptures: 1 Corinthians 6:12-21; Romans 12:1,2; 1 Corinthians 7:3,4; 2 Corinthians 6:14 - 7:1. Now list the changes God wants you to make in the use of your BODY.

> ➤ Please meditate prayerfully on the following Scriptures: Romans 12:9,10,14-21; Matthew 18:15-35; Matthew 5:21-24. Now list the names of those persons with whom God wants you to make adjustments, and next to the name, what God wants you to do.

> ➤ Write below a Solemn Covenant with God in which you give him your BODY unreservedly to be used for his glory, by LIFE or by DEATH (Philippians 1:20).

> ➤ Please sign your name here as a covenant with God.

Also, on the paper we wrote this teaching:

The Anointing With Oil

James 5:14-16 is the New Testament passage most commonly used to support the practice of anointing with oil as part of the prayer of faith for healing.

> *Is anyone among you sick? Then he must call for the elders of the church and they are to pray over him, anointing him with oil in the name of the Lord; and the prayer offered in faith will restore the one who is*

> *sick, and the Lord will raise him up, and if*
> *he has committed sins, they will be forgiven*
> *him. Therefore, confess your sins to one*
> *another, and pray for one another so that*
> *you may be healed* (James 5:14-16).

Several observations on this text should be made:

1. The suffering person himself is commanded to pray (and keep on praying, as indicated by the verb tense); verse 13.
2. The infirm or weakened person is to request the church elders to pray over him, anointing him with oil in the Lord's name; verse 14.
3. Prayer "in the name of the Lord" and "offered in faith" is receptive to whatever may be God's will. To do or say something in the Lord's name is to place one's self within the periphery of God's will.
4. The oil of anointment is non-medicinal, used symbolically for the presence of God's Spirit.
5. Some sicknesses may be due to the sin of the sufferer or sin within the church; for such sicknesses open confession is the first part of the remedy; verses 15,16.
6. Scripture indicates in a larger context that God may accomplish one of these possible results through sickness: A sickness unto:
   a. GLORY is one in which God will gain glory for himself through a supernatural healing (Luke 17:15; John 11:4).

b.   GRACE is one in which the sufferer receives added grace to cope with the physical problem so that God may grant spiritual strength (2 Corinthians 12:7-10).

c.   The GRAVE is one which is on the agenda of every human until Jesus comes and cannot be forestalled outside of God's will by any means (Psalm 89:47,48).

7.   Any healing that is effected is from the Lord. It is not the elders, nor their faith, nor the oil, nor anyone's piety, *"the Lord will raise him up;"* (verse 15).

Those who receive the healing touch of the Great Physician will not be surprised that they are healed because God most eagerly and effectively works such healing ministry in the lives of those who reach out to God in faith in all areas of their lives.

Looking to the Lord for healing is not just a matter of trusting God in one area of life. It is trusting God for everything. Those who do receive healing by faith are often people who constantly depend upon the Lord for strength and health as well as for wisdom and growth.

Gloriously Glorified

All parts of the good news, the gospel of salvation, will gloriously come together in the final phase of our Christian experience, our glorification with Jesus. *When Christ, who is our life, is revealed, then you also will be revealed with Him in glory* (Colossians 3:4). The exact nature of that glory is unknown to us now. What a great surprise we have ahead! Until that time, we are not to sit idle, longing to escape the troubles of this world. Rather, we are to enjoy and demonstrate the rest of God's glorious gospel: conversion, repentance, faith, reconciliation, redemption, justification, adoption, sanctification, and divine healing – all are part of your salvation. One wonders why it is called only good news – it is great news, the greatest!

Section Three:
The Spirit and the Church

Chapter 15

God the Spirit

Jesus said that when the Spirit would come, his greatest ministry in the church would be glorifying Jesus Christ, the Son of God, rather than calling attention to himself as the third person of the Godhead.

Perhaps because the Holy Spirit may not seem quite as personal to us as our Father in heaven or as Jesus, the Son, it is easy for us to think of him as third in importance, or perhaps as just a name we have heard in prayers and benedictions. Pastor David Pawson in England referred to this lack of emphasis on the Holy Spirit in this humorous over-generalization: The Catholics believe in "God the Father, God the Son, and God the Holy Virgin" and the Protestants believe in "God the Father, God the Son, and God the Holy Scriptures." Where is the Holy Spirit?

In the Old Testament we are confronted with God the Father, who was very personal to the Jews. He led and judged them, provided their needs, and spoke directly to them through the prophets.

In the New Testament we meet the second person of the Godhead, Jesus Christ, the personal, incarnate expression of God – God in the flesh. We hear his teachings, we see him doing many miraculous deeds, we know who his friends were, and we know very much about his life.

When it comes to the Holy Spirit, we are not given as much personal information as we might like. Perhaps this is part of God's plan. Without knowing about the Holy Spirit, though, we cannot really say that we know God, for the Holy Spirit is God!

A Power Or Person?

We want to consider now whether the Holy Spirit is a he or an it. Is the Holy Spirit a personal being or a force?

At first look we might suspect that the Holy Spirit is an impersonal force or power. Often when we think of "spirit," we do not think of a being that we can know and relate to as we would to another person; rather we think of an attitude or a power. We use expressions such as a spirit of expectancy. In so doing we are talking about a mood or a shared feeling on the part of a group. We are not talking about a personal being.

In Scripture, however, the Holy Spirit is not just a force. The pronouns used in the New Testament to refer to the Holy Spirit are in the masculine gender. If you have studied foreign languages, you may know that nouns often are given in one of three genders: masculine, feminine, or neuter. In Greek, the word for spirit is a neuter word, but whenever the Holy Spirit is referred to, the Greek pronouns used are masculine ones. In John 14, for example, Jesus called the Holy Spirit the Counselor or Comforter and said in verse 17, *The world cannot receive, because it does not behold Him or know Him, but you know Him because He abides with you, and will be in you.* Notice the pronouns *him* and *he.*

Since one cannot see the Holy Spirit and since the Holy Spirit does not have a biography in Scripture, as it were, what difference does it make whether we call the Holy Spirit by a personal pronoun or an impersonal pronoun? What difference does it make whether we consider the Holy Spirit to be a person or a power?

Actually, it makes quite a bit of difference. For one thing, if the Holy Spirit were not a person, he could not be part of the Godhead, for God is a personal being. It would be quite impossible for the Holy Spirit to be one in nature with the other parts of the Godhead if he were not a person.

On a more practical, personal level, if we consider the Holy Spirit to be only a force, we would not relate with him in the way the Bible says we should. We are cautioned, for example, not to grieve the Holy Spirit (Ephesians 4:30). We would not give that a second thought if we considered the Holy Spirit to be a force, for one cannot grieve a force. It is possible, however, to grieve the Holy Spirit, for he is a person. The Holy Spirit is also called the Comforter and a Teacher (John 14:26). These roles can be assumed only by someone with personhood.

Another evidence of the personhood of the Holy Spirit is found in his name. He is the HOLY Spirit. Holiness is a personal attribute. Holiness has to do with a standard of living. It is righteousness or moral excellence. We do not use the word *holy* to speak of forces or powers. A force, which does not have personality or will, cannot really be said to be holy. We think of a person as being holy, but we would never claim that holiness is an attribute of a tornado or a blast of dynamite or an electric shock or any other power or force which is not a person.

His Address

As a personal being, the Holy Spirit requires a place to reside. When Jesus left the earth, he promised to send the Holy Spirit to reside with or in Christians. We need to know where he actually lives. Unlike Jesus, who during his earthly existence had a local address – perhaps not a particular street number, but rather a geographical area in which he could be found – the Holy Spirit has no specific address. He lives wherever he is invited to live.

Prior to the days of Jesus, the Holy Spirit only visited the people of God, coming upon them for special events and activities. One time at a feast Jesus said, *If any man is thirsty, let him come to Me and drink. He who believes in Me, as the Scripture said, 'From his innermost being shall flow rivers of living water'* (John 7:37-38). Then John, the Gospel writer, adds this comment in verse 39, *But this He spoke of the Spirit, whom those who believed in Him were to receive; for the Spirit was not yet given, because Jesus was not yet glorified.* We learn from this verse that the Spirit of God would be given to the people of God when Jesus would be glorified, that is when he ascended into heaven after his resurrection and assumed his rightful place with God the Father. We also learn that the Holy Spirit would be given to those who believe in Jesus. They were later to receive the Holy Spirit as Jesus had promised.

The Holy Spirit dwells in the lives of people who know Jesus personally. Jesus told Nicodemus that unless a man is born again, he cannot enter the kingdom of God (John 3:5). Paul taught in Romans, *But if anyone does not have the Spirit of Christ, he does not belong to Him* (Romans 8:9). If you know Jesus Christ personally through faith, then the Holy Spirit lives within you. This is not to say that you have gone as far as you might go in your relationship with the Holy Spirit or that you have been filled with the Spirit, but you can be sure of the fact that if you are a born-again Christian, the Holy Spirit lives within you.

What's He Doing?

By picturing and comprehending the Spirit's activities, we can better understand him as a person. The Father has certain primary responsibilities in creating, sustaining, and caring for the creation. The Son is the Redeemer – the one whose life, death and resurrection have set the groundwork for restoring the creation in right relationship with the Father. What then is the work of the Holy Spirit? When we consider what the Bible says about the task given to the Holy Spirit, we see that he is indeed a very busy worker.

There are several specific works of the Holy Spirit, yet there is no set order in which these must occur for a Christian. Jesus said,

> *And He, when He comes, will convict the world concerning sin and righteousness*

> *and judgment; concerning sin, because*
> *they do not believe in Me; and concerning*
> *righteousness, because I go to the Father*
> *and you no longer see Me; and concerning*
> *judgment, because the ruler of this world*
> *has been judged. I have many more things*
> *to say to you, but you cannot bear them*
> *now. But when He, the Spirit of truth,*
> *comes, He will guide you into all the truth;*
> *for He will not speak on His own initiative,*
> *but whatever He hears, He will speak; and*
> *He will disclose to you what is to come. He*
> *will glorify Me, for He will take of Mine*
> *and will disclose it to you* (John 16:8-14).

In this passage five works of the Holy Spirit are mentioned. Even before you became a believer, the Holy Spirit was at work trying to show you your need to be right with God and helping you see that Jesus Christ is God's way of righteousness. He convicted you of sin and convinced you that Jesus, in fact, is Savior, and that through Christ's victory, the power of Satan has been broken.

In the physical absence of Jesus, it is the Holy Spirit's task to guide disciples into all truth. In doing this he does not speak on his own authority, but conveys truth that is directly from Christ through his disciples. As he does this, the Holy Spirit glorifies Jesus Christ. Actually, that is one of the most important ministries of the Holy Spirit – to glorify Jesus Christ!

More Spirit Work

The Holy Spirit is also the one by whom we are born anew, as we have seen in John 3:5. Paul mentioned a similar idea in Titus 3:5 by saying, *He (Jesus) saved us, not on the basis of deeds which we have done in righteousness, but according to His mercy, by the washing of regeneration and renewing by the Holy Spirit.* When we come to Christ, the Spirit comes to live in us. When some of the Corinthian believers were not living holy lives but were indulging in sexual sins, Paul admonished them this way: *Do you not know that your body is a temple of the Holy Spirit who is in you, whom you have from God?* (1 Corinthians. 6:19).

By coming to live within us, the Holy Spirit also seals us or marks us as belonging to God. Paul told the Ephesians, *you were sealed in Him with the Holy Spirit of promise, who is given as a pledge of our inheritance, with a view to the redemption of God's own possession* (Ephesians 1:13-14). The sealing of the Holy Spirit is a mark of God's ownership upon us until he takes us to himself.

At the moment of our coming to Christ for salvation, we are also baptized by the Holy Spirit. Paul, in recognizing and teaching this, said, *For by one Spirit we were all baptized into one body* (1 Corinthians 12:13). Notice that this baptism is into a body. This unique ministry of the Holy Spirit brings us into a corporate relationship with all others who are in the family of God by faith.

Although the Holy Spirit indwells all believers at conversion, he also wants to infill every believer. Paul told the Ephesian Christians, *Do not get drunk with wine... be filled with the Spirit* (Ephesians 5:18). The difference between being indwelt and being filled by the Spirit is an important one. When a Christian allows the Holy Spirit to have freedom, the Holy Spirit takes over the entire being and fills the Christian with himself. A filled Christian then becomes an empowered Christian. In his last-minute remarks to his disciples in Acts 1:8, Jesus said, *You shall receive the power when the Holy Spirit has come upon you.* An empowered Christian then becomes one whom the Holy Spirit can lead.

Philip the evangelist was such a Christian after the Holy Spirit came upon him. In Acts 8:29 the Spirit told Philip, *Go up and join this chariot.* Philip then went to the chariot in which an Ethiopian was reading from Isaiah. Philip led him into a living knowledge of Jesus as Savior. After that event, the narrative continues by saying, *When they came up out of the water, the Spirit of the Lord snatched Philip away...* (Acts 8:39).

The Holy Spirit wants to lead us to places and people where he can use us effectively. One way he uses us is by equipping us each with a spiritual gift. After listing many of the spiritual gifts, Paul said in 1 Corinthians 12:11, *But one and the same Spirit works all these things, distributing to each one individually as He wills.* We will discuss this in greater detail in chapter 17.

Working In You?

The tasks of the Holy Spirit discussed in this chapter can be accomplished only in and through Christian believers. He cannot work unless people are available to be used by him. As we list the tasks again, why not check off each one if you can affirm that the Holy Spirit has worked or is working in your life in that way:

1. Convicts of the sin of unbelief
2. Convinces that Jesus is the righteousness of God
3. Convinces that the power of Satan has been broken
4. Guides into all truth
5. Glorifies Jesus Christ
6. Regenerates
7. Indwells
8. Seals
9. Baptizes
10. Infills
11. Empowers
12. Leads
13. Distributes spiritual gifts

Do you want to be doing the work of God in this world? Then you and the Holy Spirit must have a right-flowing relationship, which will involve these actions in your life. Be alert to his workings in you and through you; as you sense his working within you, you will know him. By knowing him, you will know God so much better.

Chapter 16

Crisis and Process

After years of modernization in industry and technology, society has advanced so far that it seems nothing is beyond possibility. Concepts about travel and communications that a century ago seemed to be fanciful fiction, are now reality, and even outdated. But what if sometime in the next decade a dominant world government would emerge and forbid the use of electricity, petroleum and other kinds of fuel? Imagine how our world would come to a screeching halt as we would be virtually without power.

In a sense, that is what happened in church history over 1500 years ago. The church had been growing dynamically, energized by the Holy Spirit and his gifts. Everyday Christians lived with Pentecostal power, and the world was being turned upside down by the gospel. But then something – success, politics, religion, materialism, immorality – something pulled the plug of the Spirit, and the power was gone. The world entered the Dark Ages. Even the church was a dark place for centuries. Only a few times and in a few places did it seem that the electricity was turned on.

But within the past century the spiritual electricity has been rediscovered, and all over the world Christians are plugging in to the power of the Holy Spirit. A global revival is occurring, and the church of Jesus Christ is growing rapidly. Christians are being renewed by the power of the Spirit and finding ways to use their spiritual gifts and to share their faith with others.

Palace Protocol

But there are still segments of the Church that either believe the electricity is no longer available or they are afraid of it. The most dynamic Christians I know are all plugged in. They lived in perpetual revival. Jesus is very real to them, and he works powerfully through them. Worship is their language. Obedience is their politics. They are aware of the kingship of God in their lives. They have learned to live in the royal palace, displaying kingdom manners and understanding their privileged status as children of the King.

Living a sanctified life is the protocol of the palace. Sanctification is the fashion, the wardrobe of the King's family. We may be clothed in royal garments, which never become stained. But many of the King's children continue to wear their worldly rags. Holiness is available to all believers, but many think they are only slaves in the palace, not part of the royal family. It is time for all

Christians to put on the garments of righteousness, to enter into the fullness of the Spirit through sanctification.

We are not talking here about sinless perfection. First John 1:9 acknowledges that Christians sin. *If we confess our sins, He is faithful and righteous to forgive us our sins and to cleanse us from all unrighteousness.* We are instructed in Romans 6, however, not to sin purposefully or even put ourselves in a place where we are likely to sin.

We must be realistic about the fact that we still live in a sinful world, and so it is most unlikely that any believer will go throughout his or her life after conversion without committing a sin in word, thought, or action. The holiness of life we are talking about has to do with the intention of our wills.

Sanctification means to be separated or set apart for a holy purpose. It includes being separated from the world and from sin, and being separated unto God and holiness in life. The word was used in the Old Testament to talk about dedicating a sacrifice or a temple utensil for the glory of God. Sanctification always includes the concept of holiness.

To be sanctified means always to have a burning desire to be right with God. Paul wrote to the Ephesians saying that *we should be holy and blameless* (Ephesians 1:4). He told the Thessalonians that *God has not called us for the purpose of impurity, but in sanctification* (1 Thessalonians 4:7). He explained to the Colossians that it is Christ's desire that the believer should be presented *holy and blameless and beyond reproach* (Colossians 1:22). The will of God is for every believer to be sanctified or made holy.

Perhaps the best-known verse about sanctification is 1 Thessalonians 5:23, *May the God of peace Himself sanctify you entirely, and may your spirit and soul and body be preserved complete without blame at the coming of our Lord Jesus Christ.* Then there is also the glorious promise of verse 24, *Faithful is He who calls you, and He also will bring it to pass.*

Sanctified Wholly

The possibility of being entirely sanctified is not just theoretical. It is possible to be abandoned to God without reservation. This is a glorious experience not only for the exceptional, superstar saints, but it is also one that the Lord wants to see in all of his children. Just as earthly fathers want undivided loyalty from their children, so it is with our heavenly Father, who truly deserves it.

Perhaps a stickier issue than the meaning of sanctification is the timing of sanctification. When is a believer sanctified? There has been a great debate about this question, and perhaps no clear-cut, simple answer can be given. We can look at the issue, however, and come to some conclusions.

As far as God is concerned, he looks at all believers as already having been sanctified through Christ's offering. Hebrews 10:10 explains that *we have been sanctified through the offering of the body of Jesus Christ once for all.* Again, we come across the idea of our being incorporated in Christ, so all that happens to Christ happens to us as well. As far as God is concerned, we are already set apart for a holy purpose. This is consistent with what we have seen about our being made righteous by God.

In another sense, if we are honest with ourselves, we know very clearly that we are not wholly sanctified. We are not totally separated from the world unto God. In our own experience and in our own moral life we know we fall short of that ideal. Many Bible students, looking at full sanctification, would say that it is an ideal toward which we should aspire but not one that can be attained in this life. In one sense, they are right.

The Greek word for *sanctification* has a suffix, the letters *asmos.* Those letters are the customary suffix similar to our English letters *ation,* which often conclude a word that speaks of process, like education, acceleration or meditation. So it is with the word *sanctification.* It is not a one-time experience totally concluded in one instant.

Sanctification, however is not just the process of Christian growth; there is another aspect of sanctification – a crisis experience. Perhaps *ideally* we should not need a crisis experience. At conversion, a person should be taught the full implications of being a Christian – what it means to live under the Lordship of Jesus Christ, to be filled with the Holy Spirit, and to walk by the Holy Spirit day by day. Unfortunately, that often is not the case.

Most of us come to Christianity and receive Jesus Christ as our Savior without understanding the full provision of Christ for us, or the expectations of discipleship. In a sense, it is like signing a contract without reading the fine print. Many well-intentioned soul-winners are so eager to get their prospects to say yes to Jesus that all they tell them is the "getting" side of being a Christian – that is, getting forgiveness, peace with God, the hope of heaven. The demanding side is often neglected.

It may be years after conversion before we are taught the doctrine of sanctification or the implications of having Jesus Christ as Lord as well as Savior. The crisis experience that many of us have had is just an initiation into sanctification. It may be a deeply emotional experience or a revolutionary insight, but however we perceive it, we are embarking on a new path in Christian experience that leads to the cross. The sanctified life is a life of denial. It is a life of taking up one's cross and following Christ Jesus, identifying in his death – a death to self and selfish pursuit.

After The Crisis

Many believers have made the mistake of settling for the crisis experience alone. They have been taught incorrectly that, once they have had an experience with the Holy Spirit, that is all there is to it. They are entirely sanctified, they think, and can skip through life without any more need for growth or any other such experiences.

The crisis, however, is just the beginning of sanctification, which is a process that continues developing our holiness day-by-day, week-by-week, and year-by-year. It is a continual walking in the Spirit (Galatians 5:16). This part of sanctification may properly be called Christian growth or discipleship.

Sanctification ends only when glorification begins – that is, when we are glorified with Christ at his coming. Only then will the work of sanctification have reached its conclusion. Until that time we may experience steady, consistent Christian growth or times of plateaus and further crises. We may enjoy times of very rapid growth and times of slower growth, but the direction will always be toward greater holiness of life.

So, Get On With It

The important question about sanctification is not what it means or when it happens, but how do I get into this process of growth in holiness.

The first step is that of conversion. Having experienced the new birth through faith and repentance and having become certain that we are declared righteous before God and adopted into his family as sons and daughters, we then become concerned about living the way he wants us to live. If sanctification has its start in a crisis experience, does that mean we must sit back and wait until something happens to us? On the surface, it would seem as if that were the case. We really cannot manufacture a crisis experience. Trying to do so would be totally artificial.

God doesn't expect us to sit back and wait for a bolt out of the sky to hit us before we can enter sanctification. He expects us to give ourselves fully to him, asking him to begin this work in us and to bring about the conditions in our lives that will enable such a crisis experience to take place. The heart that is hungry for God will never go unfilled. God knows your heart and if you want desperately to enter into a deep experience with him, he will make sure that your need is met. Your desire must be a genuine one; you cannot expect God to honor a half-hearted desire. If you want to be holy just to see yourself above others, then you have a wrong motive that God will not honor. If you want to be holy to please him, he will certainly help you enter the experience of sanctification.

The first thing to do is to obey Romans 12:1 – present your body to God in a deliberate act of dedication and consecration as a sacrifice to him. Sanctification, of course, involves more than just the body, but for many people that is usually the source of their greatest difficulty. So, that is the place to begin. Give him total authority over your body.

Second, do a topical study in Scripture relating to the Holy Spirit. In the previous chapter, we outlined the teaching on the Holy Spirit and included many Scripture references that will help you with your study. The goal is not just to learn about the Holy Spirit, but also to talk with God about the truths that you learn. That is called meditation.

Having come into a greater understanding of the Holy Spirit, submit to God at the beginning of each day. Someone has suggested that the way to begin every day is to give all that you know of yourself to all that you know of God. Others use different terminology, asking God to fill them anew and afresh every day with his Holy Spirit. He will honor such a prayer regardless of the terminology. What this really means is that you will be saying, "Master, here am I today, ready to serve and live for you. I want to know and do your will. I want to bring glory to you."

The proof that you are being sanctified will be the changing of your nature. Your mind becomes renewed, as Paul encourages in Romans 12:2. Your will begins to be shaped by God according to his will; your affections will be placed not on things of the earth but on things above; your body will be under the discipline of the sacrificed life; your emotions will not dominate your personality but will enjoy intimacy with Jesus Christ; and your spirit will be fellowshipping and worshipping God in great freedom and joy. When you see these things in your life, you will know that God is doing the work of sanctification in you.

Altered At The Altar

Many churches have altar calls so that people may come forward seeking salvation, healing, sanctification or some other blessing from God. The value of "going forward" is never in walking down the aisle, kneeling, crying, or even praying, but in meeting God with a hungry heart. It is possible to be saved, and even sanctified, without kneeling at an altar.

The attitude of humility and submission, however, that causes one to be willing to walk down the aisle to an altar, perhaps in front of hundreds of people, is the kind of attitude that the Lord values in us when we are seeking his fullness. The benefit of going forward during an altar call is that it is a public proclamation of making a commitment to God.

Billy Graham has said that God never called a disciple to be a private follower. When others know of a commitment I have made to God, I am more responsible to live up to that commitment. I am made accountable.

If you are ever in a church service where there is an appeal made to declare publicly your desire for sanctification or the filling of the Holy Spirit, do not hesitate out of fear of people. God honors the courage that it takes to make a public commitment. That experience may be a very decisive turning point in your life. You will always be able to remember that time when God met you as you responded to his call upon your life.

On the other hand, it will not help you to run to an altar just to seek an experience if God has not really spoken to your heart. The key to all of this is being honest with God and open in responding to him any way that he prompts you.

So, make sure you are not living in the dark ages of Christianity. Plug into the power of God's kingdom. Receive the Holy Spirit in his fullness. Who is this Holy Spirit? Keep reading.

Chapter 17

Wholly Sanctified

Since we are inhabited by One described as a *Holy Spirit*, we will be greatly affected by the presence of such a holy being living within us. We have already noted that God is a threefold being. People are created in the image of God. Part of the image of God is that we also are a threefold being. Just as God is Father, Son, and Holy Spirit, each person is body, soul, and spirit. Our prayer for one another should be what Paul prayed for the Thessalonian believers: *May the God of peace Himself sanctify you entirely; and may your spirit and soul and body be preserved complete without blame at the coming of our Lord Jesus Christ* (1 Thessalonians 5:23).

My Body, His Control

Whether we human beings believe it or like it, our bodies do not belong to us. God as the Creator owns every person, every human body. As committed Christians, we will want to agree fully with God that our bodies belong to him. Christians are urged *by the mercies of God, to present your bodies a living and holy sacrifice, acceptable to God, which is your spiritual service of worship* (Romans12:1). This should not be mere passive acknowledgment that God owns and can control us, but should be a very active, willing commitment of each part of our body to the Lord.

Most modern humans would likely resent and reject the idea that they do not own themselves. We are conditioned socially to be independent. We take care of ourselves, so we think, and therefore we have the right to live as we choose, as long as we do not hurt others. The idea that someone else owns us, even the Almighty, is not a welcome thought to secular people. Youth culture, in particular, demonstrates vividly a sense of personal independence by such external evidences as body piercing and jewelry, tattoos, and drug abuse. Never does it seem to occur to such young people that when it comes to their body, they are just managers of someone else's property. Older people also demonstrate this autonomy in financial independence, over-eating, and indulging in extravagant luxury.

A few years ago one of my friends told me of the Lord's conviction and his repentance over a particular "sin" he had committed as a young man. While in the Navy in the 1950's Dick had a small anchor tattooed on his shoulder. For decades he hardly gave it a thought. Then one day he was meditating on the verses: *You are not your own; for you have been bought with a price; therefore glorify God in your body* (1 Corinthians 6:19, 20). He told me that the

Lord gently called his attention to the tattoo, and told him that he had defaced the temple of God. Now, obviously, these earthly temples will not endure, but while we live, we are to honor God with our body and recognize his ownership.

As president of a Christian college, I knew scores of students who had tattoos, so I decided to see what some of them thought about this. When I mentioned that my friend felt convicted about desecrating the temple of God, one young man, whom I knew to be a growing disciple of Jesus, exclaimed, "Desecrating? We're decorating the temple!" Clearly, it's a matter of motivation.

Of course, we can become legalistic about this, as with other issues; we have no right to judge other people. They belong to God, and we have no right to judge the servant of another. But it is certainly true that, since we belong to God, our body should reflect our desire to be good stewards of his property. This includes what we put into our body as well as what we put onto it. Chemical abuse, either alcohol or drugs, prescribed or illegal, can keep a person in bondage, but it often begins because the user has not lived under the lordship of Christ. The way of freedom is by submitting one's body to God the owner.

I think it is wise to present each part of our body to God in total dedication, especially those parts which most easily cause us to sin.

Sanctified Soul

My soul is deeply grieved, to the point of death. The most mature, healthy person who ever lived said those words (Matthew 26:38). He was talking to his closest friends in the Garden of Gethsemane. Was he suicidal? Clinically depressed? Or just being morbid? What was the condition of his soul at that time? And what did he mean by *soul*?

Perhaps the concept of the human soul is the most abstract and confusing in the Bible. In Greek thought, the soul (*psyche)* was the immaterial, immortal part of the human being. But then, what is the spirit? Jesus, as a Jewish thinker, was probably not referring to having a depressed spirit. And he certainly was not suicidal or morbid. He knew that his destiny as the Son of God would see him rejoining the Father. But before that, he would have to go through a terrible death, carrying the sins of the world, and literally going through hell before his resurrection.

Because we have adopted a tri-partite view of the human being – body, soul and spirit – we need to recognize the soul as an entity distinct from the spirit or body. I believe the soul consists of emotions, intellect, and will. And just as our body is to be yielded to the lordship of Christ, so should we present our soul to him.

Humans pass through various stages of life, and experience different struggles of soul in those stages. For example, although he was still a young man at age thirty-three, Jesus was experiencing the grief of death, which usually is experienced by older people. During that time, Jesus wanted so much to enter the deepest intimacy with the Father. And that is a common experience for people who are pondering their mortality. Having emotions under the Lord's control is important.

In the prime of life, as responsible adults, people are at their peak as decision makers. They may have children who need good counsel; they have financial responsibilities and earn salaries that require good judgment. People at work rely on them to make good decisions. Leadership in church and civic positions requires them to exercise wisdom. Submitting our will to the Lord's leadership is essential for men and women to be at their best as parents and leaders.

In our twenties, most people are developing as professionals, when they must maximize their intellectual gifts. Learning to master a job and be proficient as an employee is so important for the rest of life. By asking God to energize our mind, conforming it to his wisdom, we put ourselves in the best position for excellence.

Teenagers can easily tend to be moody persons, at least at some stages in their development. This is quite natural if we consider that young people are undergoing many physical changes and elements of growth to which they must adjust. But moods and emotions do not need to control Christian teens. It is possible to give our emotions to God.

So, it is evident that in all stages of life, it is important for our mind, will and emotions to be under the Lord's leadership, or, to say it another way, to be fully sanctified.

His Spirit Fills My Spirit

Another part of our three-fold nature is the human spirit, the part that communicates with God. In that sense, the unbeliever does not have a living, functioning human spirit. He cannot begin to communicate with God because sin alienates him from God. It is only when a person repents of his sins and comes into newness of life in Christ that the Holy Spirit gives life to his human spirit. Romans 8:16 tells us, *The Spirit Himself bears witness with our spirit that we are children of God.*

How will the Holy Spirit-filled human spirit function? One dramatic change is that we begin to engage in the highest and most notable activity of a human being; we worship God in spirit! Worshiping God is more important than any other activity, and it will continue right through all eternity.

Many Christian activities, like reading the Bible, praying, witnessing, and attending meetings, will be over and done with when we are in the Lord's presence in heaven. We will not need to read our Bible because we will be in the presence of Jesus, the Living Word. We will not need to pray, for we will have immediate communication with God. Witnessing will be unnecessary because everyone in the kingdom will already know the gospel. Church meetings will cease because we will have continual fellowship with all of God's redeemed family.

Worship, however, will continue, and will, in fact, intensify. It would be wise, then, for us to learn how to worship effectively here on earth. It could well be that many Christians will feel quite awkward in heaven because they will not have had proper attitudes and experiences in worshipping God. It is in the realm of our spirit where true worship occurs, worship that God accepts.

Some people think that certain external conditions are required before worship can be effective. Perhaps they insist on a special holy place or a particular mood to direct their spirit toward God. That really should not be the case.

While public worship is a very important activity, and contributes to our lives as Christians in a great way, private worship may be even more important. Dr. Billy Graham, interviewed at a mission conference before sixteen thousand college and university students, was asked about his own devotional life. He said that the most important thing he does on any given day is worship God. That would not be such an incredible statement for any one of us to make, but here was a man who met with presidents, emperors, and kings; who traveled all over the world talking and ministering to thousands of people at a time; and yet he confessed that the most important thing that he did on any given day was worship God.

Regardless of the busy-ness, responsibilities, or earthly position any human has, worship should be our highest priority. We were not created merely to be successful on earth; our higher calling, even before we go to heaven, is to love, know, and worship God. When we worship, we are actually growing our spirit. We are allowing our spirit to be taken over by the Holy Spirit, and thus comes the great gift of God-consciousness, though we are still living our life on earth.

Pneuma-rhythms

In our generation, there has been a renewed emphasis on recognizing the work of the Holy Spirit. While this is a good development, many strange ideas are going around because his varied ministries in our lives are not understood. People often use their experiences as more authoritative than the Scriptures regarding spiritual experience, which is often how cults get formed. Much of this "fuzzy" thinking can be cleared up by examining four concepts. It will be helpful to illustrate them.

Regeneration is the Spirit's work in which a new believer first receives the Holy Spirit. Prior to regeneration, our spiritual status looked like this: ☐ an empty box signifying no spiritual life. Regeneration, or conversion, is the beginning of spiritual life, looking like this: ☐. That experience must precede the next three, but the next three do not come in any fixed order.

Sanctification, which is usually a process of growth in holiness, is illustrated like this: ▱

At some time in a growing believer's life the Holy Spirit may break through in a very dramatic way in what is called *baptism in the Spirit.* It may occur at the time of regeneration, but for most Christians it comes later. Some, probably most, Christians do not submit to the lordship of Christ, which seems to be a prerequisite for the baptism of the Holy Spirit. In any case, Spirit-baptism is a very radical moment of tremendous growth, illustrated like this: ▱

Another experience is the *filling of the Holy Spirit.* Actually, we should speak of *fillings,* for in Acts we find the apostles filled several times for specific ministries. This is similar to a special anointing for specific service, and it will recur often in the life of an active Christian. We may picture the fillings like this: ▱

Have you ever heard of bio-rhythms, the cycle of energy levels and mood swings that people experience as part of their physical and psychological makeup? Supposedly, our body-clock determines our mood swings, health patterns, energy levels, and intellectual alertness, and these are plotted on a chart. Whether biorhythm charts present a

David E. Schroeder

true picture we cannot say, but we raise the issue to talk about "pneuma-rythms." *Pneuma* means *spirit,* so we are talking about a pattern of spiritual life. Each Christian's pneuma-rhythm chart will be distinctive, but using the four symbols for regeneration, sanctification, baptism, and filling, a pneuma-rhythm chart might look like this:

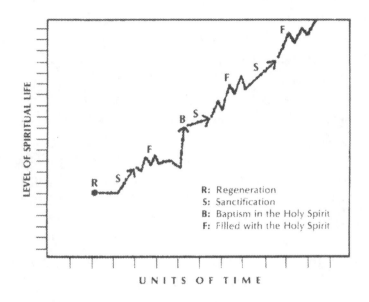

R: Regeneration
S: Sanctification
B: Baptism in the Holy Spirit
F: Filled with the Holy Spirit

In this example, after regeneration there was a short period of no growth. Then a time of growth in sanctification was followed by experiences of filling. But then came a time of no growth and even "backsliding" before the baptism in the Holy Spirit. From this time on there is continual growth in sanctification, and there are frequent fillings. This, of course, is hypothetical because there are no measurements for spirituality, but it does help us visualize the different characteristics of the four

170

concepts. By now you might already be sketching your own pneuma-rhythm chart. Go ahead, but remember where you are is not as important as the direction you are going.

Are You Filled?

Having considered that we are threefold beings and that each part of our being – body, soul, and spirit – needs to be filled with God's Spirit, we come now to the critical question of whether or not we are filled. It is not adequate to know about the Holy Spirit, who he is, what he is like, and what he can do; if we are going to be effective Christians, we need also to be filled with God's Spirit.

How is that accomplished?

Thank God, it is not a complicated procedure! Four words express the process of being filled with the Holy Spirit. First, *surrender* to him. This is what we are doing when we obey the command in Romans 12:1, to present our bodies as a living and holy sacrifice to the Lord.

Second, *ask* to be filled. God is more eager than we are for us to be filled with his Holy Spirit. Jesus said to his disciples, *If you then, being evil, know how to give good gifts to your children, how much more shall your heavenly Father give the Holy Spirit to those who ask Him?* (Luke11: 13). As simple as this sounds, many Christians never bother to ask to be filled with the Holy Spirit.

Third, *obey* God. When Peter was testifying to Jewish leaders about the resurrection of Jesus Christ, he said, *We are witnesses of these things, and so is the Holy Spirit, whom God has given to those who obey Him* (Acts 5:32). Obedience is always a sign of submission. We cannot expect God to fill us with himself if we are still filled with ourselves, wanting our way, insisting on our rights, doing our thing. We must be obedient.

Fourth, *believe* him. The Galatian Christians at one time began to backtrack on their belief. In very strong warnings Paul said, *This is the only thing I want to find out from you; did you receive the Spirit by the works of the Law, or by hearing with faith?* (Galatians 3:2). Once you have surrendered fully to the Lord, have asked for the Holy Spirit to fill you, and have begun to obey him, it is important that you believe what God has said.

Being filled with the Holy Spirit is an experience that requires faith every bit as much as your initial conversion. Once you have fulfilled the four steps, do not doubt that you are filled with the Holy Spirit. This is not to say that you will not require further fillings. Each day we should come before the Lord surrendering, asking, obeying, and believing anew and afresh to be filled with a fresh filling.

There is, however, a sense in which our initial filling is a crisis experience. Dr. A. W. Tozer, in his book, *Keys to the Deeper Life,* wrote about this aspect of filling:

Neither in the Old Testament nor in the New nor in Christian testimony as found in the writings of the saints as far as my knowledge goes, was any believer ever filled with the Holy Spirit who did not know he had been filled. Neither was anyone filled who did not know when he was filled. And no one was ever filled gradually. The man who does not know when he was filled was never filled (though of course it is possible to forget the date). And the man who hopes to be filled gradually will never be filled at all.[17]

How is it that a believer knows for sure that he or she has received the baptism of the Holy Spirit or is filled with the Spirit? While we need to exercise faith to receive his fullness, we do not need to depend only on faith to be assured of this experience. Repeatedly in the book of Acts when believers experienced the filling of the Holy Spirit, they also received a "manifestation" that confirmed his presence. Some of these are listed in 1 Corinthians 12:8-10. While we are not encouraged to seek manifestations, but to seek the fullness of the Lord himself, we can rightly expect a confirming manifestation.[18]

What is your relationship with the Holy Spirit? Is he just an abstract, impersonal part of the Godhead? Is he just a name cited in the creed? Or are you aware of being indwelled, filled and empowered for holy living and faithful ministry in the kingdom of God? We certainly cannot claim that we have much knowledge of God, nor can we claim that we are living under the Lordship of Jesus Christ if we are not eager to be filled with the Holy Spirit.

Chapter 18

Spiritual Fruit

In writing to the Corinthian believers, Paul said twice within a few chapters that Christian believers are the temple of God. Yet he was not saying the same thing in each instance. In 1 Corinthians 6:19 Paul said, *Do you not know that your body is a temple of the Holy Spirit, who is in you, whom you have received from God?* In this case, Paul was talking about each individual Christian being a residence for the Holy Spirit. This is the vertical dimension of life in the Spirit. We have already considered that relationship of the Holy Spirit with the Christian believer.

In 1 Corinthians 3:16, however, Paul asked, *Do you not know that you are a temple of God, and that the Spirit of God dwells in you?* In this case Paul was emphasizing that the Holy Spirit indwells the whole Church, particularly the relationships between the members. It is this aspect of the

Spirit's indwelling we want to consider in this chapter – the horizontal dimension.

How does the Holy Spirit relate to the Church? How does the community of believers experience the presence and power of God's Holy Spirit as the members relate to one another? In looking at this issue we will consider the fruit of the Holy Spirit and the gifts of the Holy Spirit.

Some Christians might think that these topics are the deeper areas of Christian experience. Are these issues, the fruit and gifts of the Holy Spirit, really too deep for most Christians? Are we now treading on ground that is reserved for only the most saintly and mature Christians? Should average Christians really explore these topics?

The Apostle Paul gives us encouragement at this point. He told the Corinthian believers that they did not lack any spiritual gift (1 Corinthians 1:7). Although they frequently expressed these gifts in ministry, the Corinthian church was not an extremely mature, spiritual group. Just a few chapters later Paul said, *And I, brethren, could not speak to you as to spiritual men, but as to men of flesh, as to babes in Christ. I gave you milk to drink, not solid food; for you were not yet able to receive it. Indeed, even now you are not yet able, for you are still fleshly* (1 Corinthians 3:1-3).

How can it be that a church blessed with every spiritual gift could still be worldly, carnal and immature?

We will notice as we discuss the fruit and the gifts of the Holy Spirit that while both are very important for the life of the church, ultimately it is the fruit of the Holy Spirit that shows the believer to be mature in Christ. The gifts relate to how we are oriented and to what we do. The fruit relates to who we are. The gifts have to do with the ministry; the fruit has to do with character.

From Root To Fruit

Before Jesus gave his detailed teaching about the Holy Spirit in John 16, he used the analogy of the vine and the branches in John 15. There is a definite link between the ministry of the Holy Spirit and the fruit that is produced in the life of the believer.

Often when we think of fruit in the Christian sense, we consider it to be the end result of our ministry to other people. If someone has a preaching ministry and is asked if he saw any fruit in his ministry, what he is really being asked is: "Did anyone get saved?"

This is not, however, the only biblical use of the word *fruit*. In the vine and branches metaphor that Jesus used, the owner of the vineyard would be looking for the branches to produce fruit, not just more branches. If *fruit* refers to soul-winning, the branch has merely produced another branch, not necessarily fruit. The fruit must be something that changes the character of the branch by making it more valuable. I believe that the fruit Jesus spoke about was the same that Paul mentioned in Galatians 5:22-23, the fruit of the Spirit.

Before leaving the analogy of the vine and branches, we need to see that Jesus Christ said that he himself is the true vine. It is only our connection with him that enables us to produce any fruit at all. In fact, without our connection with the vine, we have no life. We are merely dead branches, which are useless as far as God is concerned. God the Father is called the gardener in John

15, and Jesus said, *Every branch in Me that does not bear fruit, He takes away; and every branch that bears fruit He prunes it, that it may bear more fruit* (John 15:2).

Notice the two kinds of trimming that the gardener does. One is cutting off the useless dead branches that cannot bear fruit. Certainly, that is the trimming that none of us wants to experience. The other kind of trimming is called pruning. It is the cutting off of useless parts of the branch so that the full nutrition from the soil can bring greatest benefit to the parts that will bear fruit. It is the pruning process that the Lord wants to apply in our lives.

Without doubt, we can see in other people some areas where pruning is essential. Often, however, we are blind to our own dead spots, so we need the ministry of the rest of the body of Christ to help us be pruned properly. God the gardener wants to use his body to do the trimming that needs to be done in his garden. This is why the Holy Spirit relates not just to the individual Christian but also to the whole body of Christ. When we submit ourselves to the church body as unto the Lord, we are giving that body the right to admonish us, rebuke us, and do all of the other functions that will contribute to our being pruned. The ultimate goal is not to glory in any one branch, but for the entire garden to be a profitable field for the Lord's harvest.

Spiritual Citrus

Centuries ago some British sailors were found to be seriously ill. A diagnosis showed that they were lacking an essential ingredient in their diet. They had scurvy – a disease caused by a lack of certain vitamins found in citrus fruit. Thus, the British fleet began taking citrus fruit on their voyages. Even today British sailors are sometimes called "limeys."

In a sense, Christians become malnourished if they do not have adequate spiritual "citrus" in their lives. Galatians 5:22-23 lists nine kinds of fruit: *But the fruit of the Spirit is love, joy, peace, patience, kindness, goodness, faithfulness, gentleness, and self-control.*

We notice that the word *fruit* is singular, and wonder whether Paul should have used the word *fruits* rather than *fruit*. Some commentators suggest that these nine could all be produced together in the believer's life, and that when the Spirit fills us and we walk by the Spirit, all nine "flavors" of the fruit of the Holy Spirit will be produced in our lives so that we are becoming more like the character of God.

The different kinds of fruit express various characteristics, or attributes, of God. In fact, as we see below, certain attributes of God produce in us the fruit of the Spirit. As we consider the nine parts of the fruit of the Holy Spirit and what portions of the character of God they reflect, we may ask ourselves whether other people might be able to see each part of the fruit in our lives.

Our fruit	Produced by	God's attributes
Love		Love
Joy		Sovereignty
Peace		Omnipresence
Patience		Wisdom
Kindness		Mercy
Goodness		Providence
Faithfulness		Changelessness
Gentleness		Grace
Self-Control		Omnipotence

Love, Joy, Peace

Love in the New Testament is unselfish and always concerned for others. *Love is patient, love is kind and is not jealous; love does not brag and is not arrogant, does not act unbecomingly; it does not seek its own, is not provoked, does not take into account a wrong suffered, does not rejoice in unrighteousness, but rejoices with the truth; bears all things, believes all things, hopes all things, endures all things* (1 Corinthians 13:4-7). This love is a reflection of God's love. When people see this kind of love in us, they really are seeing God's love being manifest.

Joy is the deep-seated inner conviction that my life is in harmony with the will and purpose of God. This kind of joy is not the same as happiness, which always depends upon the circumstances of our lives. We may be joyful despite very unhappy circumstances of our lives. The prophet Habakkuk wrote: *Though the fig tree should not blossom, and there be no fruit on the vines, though the yield of the olive should fail, and the fields produce no food, and there be no cattle in the stalls, yet I will exult in the Lord, I will rejoice in the God of my salvation* (3:17-18).

When one is rightly related to God, he or she is able to be joyful continually. The amount of joy in our life is a measure of our confidence in the sovereignty of God. If we truly believe that our life is ordered and led by a sovereign God who loves us, the external events of life do not matter too much. Joy is the reflection of one who believes in the sovereignty of God.

Peace is a condition reflecting the presence of God in one's life. In John 14:27, after Jesus had promised that the Holy Spirit would come and remain with the Christians, he said, *Peace I leave with you; My peace I give to you; not as the world gives, do I give to you. Let not your heart be troubled, nor let it be fearful.* Peace is the calm assurance that we are accepted by God and living in his favor.

Patience, Kindness, Goodness

Patience reflects confidence in God's wisdom. It is the attitude of remaining at rest about what God will do, even though we cannot see that action immediately. James illustrated patience by saying, *Be patient, therefore, brethren, until the coming of the Lord. Behold, the farmer waits for the precious produce of the soil, being patient about it, until it gets the early and late rains* (James 5:7). Sometimes we exhibit a short temper; patience is the opposite – it is having a long temper. It is the ability to see things through without yielding to negative reactions. It is the kind of endurance needed for the long road.

Kindness reflects the mercy of God at work in a person's life. Understanding the great mercy of God in forgiving our offenses against him enables us to imitate that quality by being kind. Kindness is the sweetness of temper that puts others at ease and avoids giving pain.

Goodness expresses kindness: it reflects the providence and generosity of God. The person who is good does not merely settle for justice in the lives of people around her, but actually gives people what they need but may not deserve. She is generous, openhanded, and openhearted. Truly goodness a reflection of the character of God!

Faithfulness, Gentleness, Self-Control

Faithfulness is the quality of trustworthiness and reliability in those upon whom we can utterly depend and whose word we can totally accept and trust. Faithfulness reflects the changelessness of God. We know God is faithful, and we can confidently sing, "Great Is Thy Faithfulness" because he does not change his mind or act according to impulse.

Gentleness reflects the grace of God: it is not weakness but tamed strength. Gentleness is seen in a watchdog who is bravely hostile toward strangers but gently friendly with people whom he knows and loves. The watchdog is valuable not merely because of tremendous strength, but for knowing how to temper that strength. So it is with the gentle Christian.

Self-control reflects the power of God in the life of the believer. It is that strength of soul which enables a man to maintain full control so that he can resist and win over every evil desire. The Christian who allows God's Spirit to reign in his life will find that he has new moral strength to curb his natural desires before they give birth to sin.

So, what should I do to acquire the fruit of the Spirit? Should I work on one quality at a time until I think I have mastered it? Will this be a self-improvement effort? How long should it take? And how will I know when I am ripe? These are good questions, but they are moving in the wrong direction. Let's recall the imagery of the vine and the branches.

We Christians should be eager to see the fruit of the Spirit produced in our lives, but we cannot expect this fruit to ripen overnight. It all depends on our abiding in

Christ. We cannot bear this fruit just by being branches. The branch must remain in the vine before this fruit can be produced. It is through the vine that the branches receive nourishment and life. We must be concerned about staying in the vine. Our efforts must be directed toward abiding in Christ, not trying to polish our character in our own strength. Focus on the vine, Jesus Christ, not on the fruit, and then the vine will produce the fruit in you.

Chapter 19

You Are Gifted

Besides wanting to produce the fruit of the Spirit in your life, God also wants to trust you to minister to others. To do that, he has given you a special gift which he wants to use in the body of Christ to build up other Christians. While our salvation and eternal life are gifts from God, we are not speaking of those kinds of gifts just now but of the gifts of the Holy Spirit.

In Scripture, there are four lists of gifts. This can be somewhat confusing because the gifts are not identical in the four passages. One of the lists is in Ephesians 4, where Paul wrote about people who are gifts from God to the Church. Listed there are the functions or offices that some of God's gifted ones hold. They are apostles, prophets, evangelists, pastors, and teachers. Since it is obvious in that passage that the gifts are people, we do not necessarily refer to them as gifts of the Holy Spirit in terms of endowments or abilities given for ministry.

Gift Lists

Two lists are found in 1 Corinthians 12. Verses 8-10 actually lists manifestations of the Spirit. One of the manifestations has attached to it the word *gifts,* namely gifts of healing. These all seem to be opportunities given to Christians for ministering in various ways at different times, and are not spiritual gifts, which are motivations, not ministries or manifestations. To build a case here would take lengthy interpretation, which I have done in my book *Walking in Your Anointing,* but it can be shown that manifestations are not gifts of the Holy Spirit; they are manifestations.

The situation is a bit confused because the first verse of 1 Corinthians 12 has the word *gifts* supplied in many translations, but the Greek text actually says, *Now concerning spiritual (things) (pneumatika) or that which is spiritual.* Paul did not use *charismata*, the word for gifts. In verses 4 to 6 Paul distinguished between gifts, ministries and effects. These may be three categories of the spiritual things from verse 1. Verses 8 to 10, the manifestations, probably refer to the effects of the Holy Spirit. And it is evident that the Corinthian believers were having some problems with the manifestations, not the gifts of the Spirit, for that is what Paul writes about in chapters 12 and 14 of 1 Corinthians.

First Corinthians 12:28-30 also gives a list, which features some functions like those in Ephesians 4, and some manifestations like those earlier in the chapter.

Paul's point in verses 28-30 was to emphasize the variety of spiritual ministries and the certainty that the Church needs the ministry of all the members.

The other list is in Romans 12, where Paul clearly uses the word *charismata* to refer to seven motivations that underlie the ministries of Christians. This is the only list of spiritual gifts in the Bible. Also, here, and in several other biblical passages, it is evident that the apostle teaches that each believer has only one spiritual gift. We may have many ministries and manifestations of the Spirit, but they all flow out of one primary motivational gift, one of the ones listed in Romans 12:6-8. While the manifestations of the Spirit may seem to be more spectacular, the gifts of the Spirit are more foundational to the life of the church.

In writing to the Corinthians, Paul was trying to correct a situation in which the "gifts" (manifestations, really) were being abused, but in writing to the Romans, he was laying down his most basic teaching. He first gave his understanding of the nature of man, then described the gospel of Jesus Christ, before turning to the work of the Holy Spirit. Romans12 contains Paul's most basic teaching on the spiritual gifts. By emphasizing the gifts, I am not expressing any reservation about the validity of the manifestations of the Spirit. But the primacy of the gifts is important.

As stated above, every Christian has one of the seven gifts listed in Romans 12:6-8. We will look briefly at each one of those gifts, not necessarily expecting that you will instantly recognize which is your spiritual gift. As we consider these gifts, please remember that often a person's ministry will not be the same as his or her gift. Not all who teach, for example, have the gift of teaching. We will use the term *teacher* to refer to one with that gift. Likewise, the same will apply to our discussion of the other gifts. It should be noted as we unwrap these gifts that though we will use male and female pronouns, they are given to both genders.

Prophesying

In our day, there is great misunderstanding about the role of prophecy. Many consider the gift of the prophet to be the ability to peer down the tunnels of the future and make predictions. The prophet, however, is not a Christian crystal-ball gazer. The primary function of the prophet is to speak forth the message of God to his own people about their own lives in their own situation. The prophet is the one who begins his message with "Thus says the Lord." He is the one who brings God's truth powerfully to the attention of Christians. He is the one who is persuasive in speech and who has unusual insight into motives of his hearers.

Generally, the prophet is zealous for righteousness, for he cannot tolerate partial good or partial righteousness. He tends to minister to groups most effectively and is not always effective in personal relationships. Often a prophet will give his message through a pulpit ministry, but not always. Many times the prophet will speak very unexpectedly and his message may seem to be critical and judgmental.

A prophet needs to be careful that he does not unnecessarily wound those who are especially sensitive.

He also needs to be careful that he does not become proud about his abilities to discern and persuade.

Serving

The server has quite a different ministry in the body. Always eager to show the love of Christ by meeting very practical human needs, she seems to have a special sensitivity to the personal needs of others and is able to overlook her own personal discomfort in order to meet those needs. Servers are extremely important in the life of the Church. Often, she is a very busy person, and has a difficult time refusing any ministry. The server wants so much to meet the practical needs of people that she cannot easily say no.

She also likes to accomplish her tasks quickly, and to sense the joy of the one whom she has served and helped. Because she is eager to help other people, the server is often thought to be brash and forward – perhaps a bit pushy. Others may feel that she does not really address the spiritual needs of a person but merely the practical, everyday-life needs. She also must be aware of the temptation to be proud of her good deeds. The server functions best when she learns not to depend upon the praise of other people about her ministries.

Teaching

The teacher has a central role in the life of the Church because he clarifies truth that God has already revealed. He delights in thinking through and researching the truth of God as it is presented in Scripture, Christian books or sermons. The teacher enjoys accumulating knowledge and loves to communicate that knowledge both to groups and to individuals.

A Spirit-filled teacher is biblically oriented and careful about his use of Scripture, often correcting those who misinterpret it. The teacher needs to be careful that he does not depend upon his own intelligence or his own mastery of knowledge as the source of his ministry. He must depend upon the Holy Spirit's ministry.

The teacher, unfortunately, may have a difficult time maintaining a consistent devotional life; his head often gets in the way of his heart, we might say. He also is vulnerable to pride of the knowledge he has accumulated and his ability to communicate that to others. He also can become bogged down in concentrating on small details of Scripture rather than communicating the basic life principles that will give the greatest help.

Exhorting (or Encouraging)

The exhorter encourages and builds others by helping them see the possibility of growth in their own lives. She is eager to encourage the faith of other Christians by describing particular actions that can be taken to promote growth. Literally, *exhort* means to call someone to the side to urge him to pursue a course of conduct. Consequently, the exhorter may often have an effective counseling ministry to individuals.

Usually the exhorter is more effective in small group settings and in one-on-one encounters than in large groups. In her counseling ministry, she will not only help people to sense the possibility of growth, but may also prescribe ways of approaching that possibility.

The exhorter often helps people understand how God is speaking to them through discouragement and adversity. She helps them use such experiences to deepen their faith rather than deepen their depression. The exhorter uses Scripture in a very practical way by looking at it topically and seeing how all the teaching of Scripture relates to the issue at hand in the life of the other person.

The exhorter needs to be careful that she does not become discouraged when the progress of others is slow. She may tend to expect too much too soon in the way of results. She also needs to be careful that she does not become proud when good results are achieved in other people's lives.

Giving

The giver is deeply motivated to earn and then entrust finances to others for the furtherance of their ministry. He tends to organize his financial interests in order to gain more funds for the work of the Lord. The giver enjoys giving what he has, but is very careful about how he does it because he is concerned about his stewardship – the making of wise investments in the Lord's work.

The true giver does not seek public recognition. He wants to obey the Lord's word about not doing his alms in public. He is quite alert to the financial and material needs of others, and his gifts usually are generous and of high quality. He has a concern to feel that he is a part of the ministry to which he contributes.

The giver must be careful not to use his financial resources to manipulate others or to buy their appreciation. He also must be careful not to judge others because they may not seem to be as generous as he is. Often a giver will tend to measure spiritual success by the way the Lord blesses materially. Since wealth is not a stamp of approval, the giver needs to be careful about this. Certainly, pride is the enemy of this gift, as well, so the giver needs to realize that all he has comes from and belongs to the Lord!

Managing

The sixth gift goes by several different names – organizing, leading, or administrating, but the term managing seems to sum it up best because it is the motivation to coordinate the activities of others for the achievement of common goals. People with this gift supervise others to accomplish big projects.

The manager is often a leader who is able to sense the long-range goals of the group and to organize ministries and efforts toward the accomplishment of those goals. The manager often has an uncanny ability of knowing the assets that are available to her in personnel and materials, and she is eager to delegate responsibility to those who are trustworthy. She is not necessarily a person who quickly grabs the opportunity to be a leader. She may allow others to do what they can until her gift is needed.

Sometimes the manager may seem to be demanding and not sensitive to the limitations of others. She may be more task-oriented than people-oriented. While it is true that she enjoys seeing all the pieces come together, the projects themselves should not really be as important to her as the people involved.

The manager may easily be misunderstood and often must endure negative reaction from those whom she is leading. They may think she carries too much authority, or suspect that her purpose in delegating responsibility is to avoid work herself.

The danger associated with this gift is the misuse of power. The manager can be proud of her influence over others and may be found to be using people to get the work done rather than "using work to get people done." This is a very important concept. The Lord's type of leadership was always people-oriented rather than task-oriented.

Mercy (Empathizing)

To empathize means to identify with and comfort those who are in distress. The empathizer is able to relate on an emotional level with people and minister to them in weeping and rejoicing. To have empathy means to feel along with someone. In fact, it is more than feeling sorry for them; it is actually feeling the pain they are experiencing as well.

The empathizer is someone who quickly detects joy or distress in either an individual or a group. He readily gravitates to those who are in distress, desiring to remove the hurts and to bring healing.

It is difficult for the empathizer to be firm, so he often becomes distressed with those who are not as softhearted as he is. This lack of firmness may appear to others as weakness and indecisiveness, as though his emotions guide him, rather than logic or the Word of God.

Since the empathizer is attracted to those in distress, he often will side with the underdog, becoming judgmental about others who may be part of that person's problem. An empathizer needs to be careful that he does not take upon himself the very problem that he is trying to solve in the other person. He needs to be careful that he does not resent others who are not as sensitive as he is.

Again, the problem of pride may creep into this gift, since the empathizer is often someone that other people will open up to quite easily. The empathizer may feel good about being the kind of person he is and even be proud of it. The empathizer is also most prone to co-dependencies.

A Gift That Fits

This discussion of spiritual gifts is not intended just to rouse your curiosity. It is a good thing to know your spiritual gift; God will reveal that to you when he chooses to do so. Not knowing your gift, however, will never keep you from ministering. Many godly people have gone throughout their lives serving the Lord faithfully and effectively without being able to say, "I am an exhorter," or "I am a prophet." It is always better to seek the Giver than the gift.

Ultimately, God's concern is not just that we as individuals know our gift and have joy ministering; we must remember that he is building a temple, and we are parts of that temple. Someone may be a brick, another a window, another a roof tile, another a pillar. There is no glory in any part of the temple. The glory is in the presence of God in the midst of all parts of the temple. We must never isolate ourselves or our spiritual gifts from the body of Christ.

It is God's desire that his glory be seen in us as individuals rightfully taking our places in the body of Christ and ministering effectively in our unique way, but never doing so for selfish reasons. The Lord wants to build a temple, and he has included you in his plan. He deems it far better for each of us to be concerned about fitting in well with his plan than to worry about whether or not anyone else notices what beautiful parts of the temple we are!

Chapter 20

Christ's Church

To a question from a new acquaintance, "What line of work are you in?" a well-known English preacher replied that he was a pastor of a church.

The man responded by saying that it must be sad to work for a "dying" organization.

The alert pastor replied, "You must be joking; don't you know that fifteen people become Christians every minute? That is an increase of more than 20,000 new "customers" every day. Surely you would be happy for that kind of growth in your business, wouldn't you?" The pastor could not resist adding: "And besides that, the Christian church is the only organization that never loses any members through death!"

It may sound preposterous, but it is true – the Church of Jesus Christ is always growing. Since that conversation in the1970's, the growth rate has exploded, resulting in

"Every day now the average number added to the body of Christ worldwide averages 174,000 … 3500 new churches are opening every week worldwide."[19]

Defining Church

One thing the pastor said may be somewhat questionable; he called the Church an organization. Now certainly there are organizations within the Church – such things as denominations, mission boards, and student groups. But the Church in its entirety is neither an organization nor an institution. It is an *organism*, a living, growing body. It is God's idea, part of his plan, his eternal family.

The word *church* is commonly used in four different ways. Sometimes we use the word church to refer to the building where Christian meetings are held. Technically, this is not a correct use of the word, because the church is not a building; it is people.

Sometimes it refers to a local church, a certain group of people who meet to worship God, learn from his Word, and fellowship with each other. Someone might say, for example, "I belong to Central Church of Milwaukee," meaning she is a member of a certain group of people who gather in Milwaukee for Christian meetings.

The word *church* is also used to refer to a group of local churches that comprise a denomination. So, we may refer to the Southern Baptist Convention as being a church, or to the Methodist church, or Presbyterian church.

Membership in both the local church and the denomination will expire one day, but there is another kind of church in which membership is eternal. It is the historic and global church, which includes all the people throughout history who trust(ed) God for salvation. That is what the word *catholic* means in the Apostles' Creed. The universal Church consists of all people who are truly born again through faith in Jesus Christ. Even some people who lived before the earthly life of Jesus are in the Church because of their faith.

More Precisely

Because *church* is such a common and often misunderstood concept, let us think more carefully about its meaning. The Greeks used the word *ekklesia* to speak of an assembly. It may have had nothing to do with religion. The Greek Senate, for example, was an *ekklesia*, a group summoned for a specific purpose. In a Christian context, the word means *God's people called together by God in order to listen to or act for God.*

What is a church? And what should it be doing? Is the goal only to get a lot of people together who like to sing hymns, listen to sermons and eat pot-luck meals? Hopefully, not. If the church is a living, growing spiritual organism, how should it be built? As with the construction of a building, we must proceed orderly.

There must be a foundation for this church. We have that. *For no man can lay a foundation other than the one which is laid, which is Jesus Christ* (1 Corinthians. 3:11). This building program is spoken about in other Scriptures, too. The Living Bible's account of Ephesians 2:20-22 says, *having been built upon the foundation of the apostles and prophets, Christ Jesus Himself being the corner stone, in whom the whole building, being fitted together is growing into a holy temple in the Lord.* With the Lord Jesus Christ and the apostles and prophets undergirding us, we surely have a strong base on which to be built.

Ephesians 2 goes on to say, *in whom you also are being built together into a dwelling of God in the Spirit.* In other words, we are like separate pieces of material, like bricks and boards and tiles. But the Builder, the Lord himself, who said, *I will build my Church,* assembles all the parts in the right relationship. The Apostle Peter called us *living stones,* which when mortared together make the walls of the Church.

More Stones

Some of the great cathedrals and temples of the world have taken hundreds of years to be built, and some are not yet finished. The Cathedral of St. John the Divine in New York City, which is longer than two football fields, was left uncompleted for thirty years until recently when the building program resumed in the 1980's. The magnificent structure still stands complete, even though it is used as a house of worship regularly.

The Church of Jesus Christ is also incomplete even though the Lord has been building it for thousands of years. The foundation is set, the cornerstone has been laid, and many of the stones are in place. God's spiritual temple, however, will not be completed until the last stone is in place.

Because people are the *living stones* in Scripture, more people will be added to the Church before it will be finished. Who are those people? They are ones who willingly want to be set upon the foundation of Christ

Jesus and the prophets and the apostles, and who also want to fit into the rest of the building. Some of them may be your friends, relatives, and neighbors. They are also people of every nation, race, and language. God is the only One who has seen the blueprint of his temple, so only he knows how many more stones need to be added. Many amateur "architects and builders," however, suspect that it will not be long before the last stone is in place, and they may be right.

Which Stones?

You may wonder, "How does God know which stones to use?" We might find the answer by thinking about what a temple is. A temple is a place where God can dwell. While God does not live in any man-made building, he does set his presence in a special way in a place prepared for and dedicated to him. He promised that to the Israelites after they had finished Solomon's magnificent temple.

> *Now it came about when Solomon had finished building the house of the Lord, and the king's house, and all that Solomon desired to do, that the Lord appeared to Solomon a second time, as He had appeared to him at Gibeon. The Lord said to him, "I have heard your prayer and your supplication, which you have made before Me; I have consecrated this house which you have built by putting My name there forever, and My eyes and My heart will be there perpetually* (1 Kings 9:1-3).

The temple that God is building now is made of people, so the only way he can live in that temple is to live in the individual stones. The stones he chooses are the ones in which he is invited to live. In other words, the people who make up the church are those who are truly Christians by having asked God to come into their lives and who by their faith in Jesus Christ are made holy through the forgiveness of their sins. God will not live in an unholy place. If you are made righteous by God, and he is living within you, then you are one of the living stones of the Church.

Our Task?

What should the Church be doing? If you live in a city and stroll down a street where there are many church buildings, you might come away quite confused if you read the notice boards. Some might say, "Gigantic Bazaar! Bargains Galore!" Another might say, "Keep Fit--Yoga Lessons on Tuesday" or perhaps "Hear the Prodigals, a New Rock Band." You would be right in wondering what all that has to do with God.

The primary task of the Church is to be a worshiping community. When we gather in the name of Jesus, we should not be too concerned about whether we get blessed, have fun, or learn anything exciting. Rather, we want to glorify and bless God, for he enjoys being with his people, expressing his love to them and hearing their words of love to him.

Another thing the Church should be doing is serving those outside the Church. We will want to be God's agents of love to the poor, lonely, handicapped, elderly, abused, imprisoned, and unsaved people around us. We will want that love to be sent around the world personally through our sending missionaries and financially through our giving.

The Church should also be fellowshipping, building up one another. We will want to help each other grow stronger spiritually. The New Testament talks a lot about "one another" relationships. We are to serve, encourage, exhort, admonish, edify, honor, and love one another. So, the Church's job is to love the Lord our God through worship, love our neighbors as ourselves by serving, and love one another as we fellowship.

You Are Summoned

If the Church is not a place we go but the people in whom God lives, is it so important that we attend church services regularly? This good question has a good answer. Let us remember that the Church is God's people called together by God. If God wants us to get together, we are disobeying him when we refuse to do so. But besides that, God enjoys the Church's corporate worship, which means his whole body (of a local church) meeting together to praise him.

Through church meetings, we are also trained and equipped to serve God in the world. It is in the church meetings that we often have edifying Christian fellowship. So, there are plenty of good reasons for obeying God's command found in Hebrews 10:25, *Not forsaking our own assembling together, as is the habit of some, but encouraging one another; and all the more, as you see the day drawing near.*

A Christian who does not desire to attend church gives a sure signal that he has the wrong idea about church. He may refuse because he does not feel he "gets anything out of it," not realizing that we should come to church to give, not to get.

On the other hand, he may think that the church is full of hypocrites, and he does not want to associate with them. What this really says is that he wants a perfect church. Someone has said, "If you ever find a perfect church, don't join it; you'll ruin it!" That is true because the church is made up of sinners. To expect a church without any hypocrites is like looking for a hospital without any injured or ill people.

Still, other people refuse to go to church because they are just too lazy; it is an inconvenience to them. They are hardly worthy of the name *disciple* if they are not willing to discipline themselves in this way. There may be other excuses for not going to church, but aside from Christians who cannot possibly go to church for health reasons, all Christians should try to be in a local assembly (church) every week.

Which Church?

If all churches are just groups of sinners gathering to worship God and learn from his Word, then it should not matter which church we attend, should it? Let us go back to the analogy of a hospital. All hospitals have as their stated purpose the care and healing of the injured and ill. Not all hospitals, however, are equal in their ability to help people. So it is with churches.

If the chief surgeon of a hospital, for example, did not believe in using the X-ray equipment, would you want to go there if you broke your arm and needed it set? Many churches that use the name *Christian* do not believe in God's "X-ray machine" that tells us what is wrong with us and how to get better; they do not believe the Bible is God's inspired, authoritative Word. If you go to a church like that, you may hear good music and nice stories, but you will not hear the gospel or the other important truths from God's Word which help you grow as a Christian. Some churches actually may be more harmful than helpful, so it really does matter which church you attend.

It is a sad but true fact that many churches in America today do not treat the Bible as God's Word, so we need to be very careful in choosing a church. It would be helpful to have an honest, personal talk with the pastor of a church before choosing it as a place to worship. Most churches subscribe to one of the historic creeds, but many of them interpret phrases to their own liking rather than what is taught in the Bible and meant by the church fathers.

Most likely, you have met many people who go to church and may even be members of a church but who have not been born again because their church does not teach the need for being born again. If they are not born again, then God's Spirit does not live in them, which means they are not really part of the Church at all, regardless of the local organization to which they might belong.

Some truly born-again Christians may feel called to attend and serve in a church that does not faithfully teach the Bible, but this is probably an exceptional calling. Usually, we will grow best in an environment where God's Word is faithfully preached to members who are Spirit-filled worshippers of the Lord and growing disciples of the kingdom of God.

Chapter 21

Church Life

We have seen that it is important that we attend church, and it is important which church we attend. But we have also seen that one of the primary reasons for gathering together is to worship God. Now, we ask the question, what should a worship service be like? Is there a set pattern for corporate worship?

The honest answer to that question is "No." The Bible tells us a lot about worship, but not much about the form or ceremony to be used. Most teaching on worship concerns our attitudes. Worship means recognizing and declaring the worth of God. The issue, then, is how can we best recognize and declare God's worth in a church service? The answer will vary somewhat with individual churches, but there are common features that will help every group of Christians desiring to worship God meaningfully.

We must come into God's presence recognizing who he is; we should come with a sense of awe or wonder about God. If we do not have that sense, then church will be merely entertaining, at best, or boring, at worst. All parts of the worship service should be planned to enhance that sense of wonder because all parts of the service should invite and expect his presence.

Unfortunately, our minds are often caught up in wander rather than wonder because we come into God's presence without preparing for worship. The details of the service may also distract us rather than lead us into true worship. Now, you may not be in a position to plan the worship service, but you are responsible to prepare your own heart for worship. Truthfully, if your heart is prepared to worship God, you will experience his presence no matter what the service is like. You can never blame anyone else for your own failure to worship God.

High Or Low?

Meaningful worship should be as God-centered as possible. There will be worship leaders who announce hymns, offer prayers, and read Scripture, but our concern must be for all glory and attention to be directed to God. Some churches have a "high" form or worship, one that is formal and liturgical. Liturgical worship can be beautiful and effective in helping people sense the majesty of God. One benefit of such worship is the connection through the creeds and lectionary with the Church through the ages. Liturgy can be beautiful and meaningful; it can also be boring and pedantic, depending on the heart of the worshipper.

Generally, evangelical churches do not follow a high form of worship. Some people who hold to a lower form of worship are mistrustful about written prayers and pre-selected hymns and readings. This is unfortunate. There is nothing unholy about being careful and orderly in planning our worship. The Holy Spirit can inspire a worship leader just as well on Wednesday when he plans the service as lead him extemporaneously on Sunday during the service. God cares only about the heart attitude of the worship leaders and worshipers.

Many Christians prefer a more informal worship service, often with greater participation by the body. Most evangelical churches have a rather set pattern of worship, but not a great deal of liturgy. Even when the church has an excellent team of pastors, there ought to be opportunity in the life of the church for lay ministries. This is a legitimate concern, which many churches recognize.

Some of the more charismatic and Pentecostal churches are open to all the members exercising spiritual gifts and manifestations publicly during the worship. This can lead to abuse like what occurred in the church at Corinth, but that is not a reason to prohibit such expression. It is far better to have all the members ministering to one another than to have only one professional minister and the rest of the people as spectators. Whatever worship style is chosen, we must be very careful that God is really at its center.

Three Cs

Ideally, every Christian should have three kinds of experience with other Christians: cell, congregation, and celebration. A *cell* is a very small sharing group. Two to five people may compose a cell, with all meeting frequently to help each other grow. Very personal matters may be shared and prayed about in such a group. Transparency and accountability are features that work better in a cell group than in larger contexts.

A *congregation* may include up to twenty or thirty people who will probably meet in a home to study the Bible, pray together, and provide each person an opportunity to get to know a few people well, be cared about personally, and help build up others. Biblical fellowship *(koinonia)* can be a rich part of the congregation's experience, as members get to participate freely in ministering to one another.

In the case of *celebration*, the more people the better, because here the purpose is to focus on God by celebrating the great biblical truths, praising God in song, receiving teaching, and observing the Lord's ordinances. If Christians have the other two "C" experiences, it will not be important that everyone in the celebration group knows everyone else. In fact, in South Korea, more than a million people gathered on the runway of an airport to worship the Lord together.

Come, Let Us Worship

If it is true that the most important thing any person does is worship, that is true also about the church. Worship means to express to God and others how great he truly is. No doubt there are people in every church who attend each Sunday and just go through the program without really making contact with God personally.

For example, wouldn't it be interesting to take a quick poll right after singing a hymn to find out how many people knew what they just sang? Did the words ever get beyond their lips to their mind, and to their heart? Were they really singing to God or just daydreaming?

Likewise, wouldn't it be interesting to find out after an offering how many people, when they put their tithes or offerings in the plate, consciously worshipped God as they gave. In their hearts were they thanking God for his faithful provision for their needs and acknowledging that their gifts are just symbols of God's ownership of all that they have? Or were they just putting money into the "collection" because the church has to pay its bills? These kinds of questions are challenging, but very important.

Worship is never just an act; it is always an attitude that expresses itself in an act. The act, without the attitude, is acting. So, when we try to describe what a worship service should be like, we must insist that it be filled with heartfelt praises for God the Father, God the Son, and God the Holy Spirit. The order of service, instruments used, style of music, etc., are just cosmetics if worship does not come from the heart.

Wordless Speech

Many things the church does, like receiving members, having meetings, listening to messages, are things also done by other groups. The local Rotary Club or Garden Club sponsors weekly meetings that can be quite similar in activities to the local church's agenda. But the church does a few things that no other group does or can do.

Some churches call them sacraments; other churches call them ordinances.

Basically, an ordinance (we will use that term here) is symbolic language, or wordless speech. It is an act that is a visual statement. Augustine, a fourth-century theologian, said an ordinance was an outward and temporal sign of an inward and enduring grace. He also said that there are only two ordinances: baptism and the Lord's Supper. Later, churchmen added other ordinances; today in the Roman Catholic Church there are seven sacraments. The Protestant reformers, however, went back to the view of Augustine, and that is the view held by most Protestant churches today. Our ordinances, then, are baptism and communion, which we will now consider.

Initiated Just Rite

Baptism is not a uniquely Christian event, because it predated Christianity. You will remember that John the Baptist was baptizing repentant Jews in the Jordan River before Jesus even began his ministry. Also, before that, Gentiles who wanted to enter the Jewish religion as proselytes had to be baptized.

In the first century, there were many cults, which had some rather bizarre practices of baptism. One group used the bull as its religious symbol, and put their converts into a pit, then covered it with a strong lattice to support the weight of the bull, which would be slaughtered. The blood then would pour down through the lattice onto the person to complete the baptismal act.

Fortunately, Christian baptism is simple and direct, a symbol of burial and resurrection. But like a Jewish or pagan baptism, it is an initiation ritual. There are several ways of baptizing, but before we consider the differences, let us look at the basics of baptism on which nearly all Christians agree.

An initiation rite is an experience which one goes through in order to join an order or a group. College guys join fraternities through initiation. Christian baptism is the initiation rite which symbolizes that one has become a Christian. Some churches baptize babies, and by doing that, they are expressing the parents' desire that their child will grow up in the Christian faith.

There is no evidence in the Bible that babies were baptized. Rather, it appears that believer's baptism was the practice of the early church; only a person who had made his or her own choice to follow Jesus Christ was baptized. However, it is an argument from silence since, for example, we do not know the ages of the household of the Philippian jailer's family who were baptized with him, as recorded in Acts 16.

Some people wait for years after they become a Christian to be baptized. Normally, it should not be that way. Baptism is not an experience reserved for a matured and fully sanctified Christian; it is for the new Christian to express his or her new commitment to God through faith in Jesus Christ. Some churches, including the early church, provide *catechesis*, biblical teaching, to prepare new believers for baptism.

Perhaps the only exception to a Christian's being baptized soon after conversion would be in the case of young children who have invited Jesus into their hearts but cannot yet understand what it means to be a disciple of the

Lord. In those cases, it might be wise for their parents to delay baptism until the child is older. This is not a biblical rule, just a suggestion. Many parents choose to wait until their children become teenagers before encouraging them to be baptized.

Buried Alive

One of the clearest teachings about baptism is found in Romans 6:3-4: *Or do you not know that all of us who have been baptized into Christ Jesus have been baptized into His death? Therefore we have been buried with Him through baptism into death in order that as Christ was raised from the dead through the glory of the Father, so we too might walk in newness of life.* While some churches baptize by pouring water from a pitcher or sprinkling water from a font, the symbolism of baptism is best expressed by total immersion in a baptistery, a lake, or river.

However, immersion is not the only valid method of baptism. As with worship, what is in the heart of the believer is most important. Immersion has the advantage of demonstrating that baptism is a symbol of death to an old life, the life of sin and selfish living, and being buried with Christ so that his sinful life dies the death of Christ's crucifixion that put him in the grave.

No one, however, stays submerged in the tank; the rest of the symbolism has to do with resurrection. As Christ was raised to a new life, so are we. That new life is the Christ-centered life that Paul spoke about in Galatians 2:20: *I have been crucified with Christ and it is no longer I who live, but Christ lives in me; and the life which I now live in the flesh I live by faith in the Son of God, who loved me, and delivered Himself up for me.*

Better Than Wetter?

Baptism, like any other spiritual activity, can be conducted merely as an external ritual without sincerity and reverence. It is possible in baptism to come out different in only one way – wetter. But just getting wet is not the purpose of baptism. So, what should our heart attitude be when we are being baptized? With regard to God, we should view it like a covenant, a determination to live wholeheartedly for Christ. With regard to ourselves, we should see it as a turning point, the beginning of our transformation into the character of Christ.

With regard to the Church, we should be making a visual, public testimony that we have received Christ into our life and that they can expect to see us living for him. With regard to the world, we should consider baptism as our "coming out party," our statement to the world that we will no longer live for it but have changed our citizenship to the kingdom of God, and that everyone should be able to know that. Baptism should never be a private affair; it is always a public statement that we are new persons in Christ and have set our course to follow him.

The Memorial Meal

The other Christian ordinance is the Lord's Supper, sometimes called Communion or the Eucharist. You might recall that after the Lord led the children through the Red Sea behind Moses, a memorial meal for the Jews was established. It was called the Passover so they would remember that the angel of death had passed over them when he slew the Egyptians. Part of that meal was eating a roasted lamb to remind them that the blood of slain lambs covering their doorposts kept the death angel from visiting judgment on their homes.

Centuries later, Jesus Christ as the Lamb of God was sacrificed so that all those who are under the protection of his blood are saved. We also have been given a sacred meal to remember our salvation. Jesus gave this meal to his disciples to remind them often of his broken body and his shed blood. He never said how often we should eat this meal, but he wanted it to be done regularly in remembrance of him. Perhaps it is the most sacred experience we have in our churches.

What is the meaning of communion? In a sense, the word *communion* repeats itself. There are two parts to the word: the first part *com* means *with* (from the Latin *cum*); the second part *union* means *together*. So, the word means "with together." In other words, communion means a total oneness in sharing, a deeply intimate experience.

In communion, with whom are we communing? What is the purpose for this "with togetherness?" We said before that it is a memorial meal, but it is not to be a somber, melancholy tribute to a dead hero. Jesus is alive; he is present at the meal; and he is, in fact, the host of the meal, so our communion is first of all with him. It is a memorial only in the sense that we are called to remember what he did for us, not in the sense that he is deceased. We need to be aware of his presence and to be communing with him while we partake of the elements.

Our communion is also with other Christians. Communion should not be a private affair; like baptism, it is a community experience. The Greek word for communion in Scripture is the same word that is used for *fellowship*. Both words mean *sharing*. We are to be very conscious of each other at the Lord's Supper. We are to be one in spirit with no faulty relationships among us. As with one mind, we are to focus on the meaning of the elements we eat. Communion dare not be done as a mere ritual; it is not a crackers and juice party!

We need to be most serious, reflective, and reverent when we take Communion. We are told in Scripture to examine ourselves before we partake. If we have ill feelings or a grudge or resentment toward anyone, we should not take the meal until we have confessed that and restored the relationship. But we can also be joyful during Communion. How could we not be joyful? Communion reminds us that our sins are forgiven, that Jesus paid for my forgiveness, that he is alive and will return. Truly, communion is more than a ritual; it is a celebration.

We need to remember that Communion is only for the believer, for those who are committed to Jesus Christ. He fed the multitudes with fish and loaves, but the wine and bread he has given only to his disciples.

The Last Church, At Last

Are you a disciple of Jesus? If so, the ordinances of baptism and communion are for you. As you participate in them, you will be aware of the Lord's presence, and you will be linking up spiritually with all of God's people. That is what being part of a Christ's Church is all about. As we observe the ordinances now in our local assemblies, we may not be aware of the total body of Christ, but a day is coming when we will celebrate together at a great banquet with all of God's redeemed people.

Jesus promised the twelve disciples that he would not drink of the fruit of the vine again until he drank it anew with them in the kingdom of God. Perhaps that will be at the wedding supper of the Lamb referred to in Revelation 19:9. On that great occasion, God's building program will be completed. Every living stone will be in place. Christians will all be gathered in God's "forever family." Until that day, each of us should do all we can to help our own local church be a place where the Lord is honored and his people are blessed.

Endnotes

1 Millard Erickson, *Introducing Christian Doctrine*, (Grand Rapids, MI: Baker Publishing Group, 1993.)

2 Wayne Grudem, *Systematic Theology*, (Grand Rapids, MI: Zondervan, 1994.)

3 A. W. Tozer, *The Knowledge of the Holy: The Attributes of God: Their Meaning in the Christian Life*. (Harrisburg, Pa: Christian Publications, 1961)

4 See Don Richardson's *Eternity in Their Heart*, (Grand Rapids, MI: Baker Publishing House, 1981.) Early "prophets" in Gentile nations testified to one, eternal, invisible, all-powerful Creator God, including Epimenedes of Knossos (Crete) and Pachacuti (1438–1472), builder of Machu Picchu in Peru. Richardson cites early God-seekers among the Chinese, Canaanites, Egyptians, Greeks, Indians, Incans, and Islands people. Could any of these people have been saved before the Messiah came? And without the Law of Moses? How was Abraham saved? Melchizedek?

5 Ernst Lange, in *Neues geistreiches Gesangbuch*, by Johann A. Freylinghausen, 1714 (O Gott, du Tiefe sonder Grund); translated from German to English by John Wesley, *Collection of Psalms and Hymns* (Charleston, South Carolina: 1737), number 16

6 A. W. Tozer, *The Knowledge of the Holy*. (New York, NY: Harper Collins Publishers, 1961.)

7 About 6 billion copies of the *Bible* are in print, whereas the next most circulated books are *The Sayings of Chairman Mao* and the *Quran*, both believed to be about 800 million. Cervantes' *Don Quixote*, first published in 1612, about 500 million, and *A Tale of Two Cities* by Charles Dickens, published in 1859 with about 200 million, are the most circulated non-religious books, according to Huffingtonpost.com.

8 See Exodus 19:5, 6; and two of the "Servant Songs" of Isaiah in 42:1-7 and 49:1-6.

9 See John Wick Bowman, *First Century Drama*. (London: Westminster Press, 1968.)

10 For a lengthy, informative, scholarly article, see Robert C. Newman, "The Council of Jamnia and the Old Testament Canon" in *Westminster Theological Journal* 38.4 (Spr. 1976) 319-348. Copyright © 1976 by Westminster Theological Seminary.

11 Well beyond the boundaries of this book is the discussion of creationism versus Darwinian evolution. Readers are encouraged to find responsible sources that do not dogmatically affirm either point of view without considering varying legitimate interpretations of Genesis 1-2 and the growing scientific uncertainties of Darwin's version of evolutionary theory.

12 Historical heresies that plagued the early Church disputed the dual nature of Jesus. Most troubling were: Docetism, which said that Christ was not a real human being and did not have a real human body. He only seemed to be human to us. Arianism taught that Jesus Christ was a special creation by God for man's salvation. A version of Arianism called Socianism said that Jesus was just an extraordinary man. This heresy lives on in two very different forms, the Unitarians and the Jehovah's Witnesses.

13 Several contemporary Christian apologists, including Josh McDowell, *Evidence That Demands a Verdict*, Frank Morison,

Who Moved the Stone, and Lee Strobel, *The Case for Christ,* expose these false opinions of Jesus.

14 Paul Little, *Know Why You Believe.* (Downers Grove, IL: InterVarsity Press, 1968.)

15 Robert Morison, *Who Moved the Stone.* (Grand Rapids, MI: Zondervan, 1958.)

16 For example, A. B. Simpson, founder of The Christian and Missionary Alliance, and Aimee Semple McPherson, founder of The Foursquare Gospel Church.

17 A. W. Tozer, *Keys to the Deeper Life,* (Grand Rapids, MI: Zondervan, 1957.)

18 More explanation about *manifestations* can be found in my book *Walking in Your Anointing.* (Bloomington, IN: AuthorHouse, 2007.)

19 "Growth of the Church – The Traveling Team," www.thetravelingteam.org

Printed in the United States
By Bookmasters